© Carl Cleves 2021

Carl Cleves has asserted his right to be identified as Author of this work

Photographs are from the author's personal collection

All rights reserved. No part of this publication may be reproduced or transmitted in any form or by any means, electronic or mechanical, Íretrieval, without prior permission in writing from the author.

ISBN 978-0-6451360-0-5

DANCING
WITH
THE BONES

Carl Cleves

'All I needed for the mind
was to be lead to new stations.
All I needed for the heart
was to visit a place of greater storms.'

- *Patti Smith*

For Parissa

'Triptych paintings and stained glass windows have hung for centuries in all the Catholic churches of my youth in Belgium. The stories they told appealed to me, and I have adopted the format in this book. Three panels, three stages of a life in a search for roots and belonging, mixing memories, dream sequences, travel and touring diaries, occasionally interrupted by the storyteller pulling the readers back into the present, where all things really happen.'—*Carl Cleves*

CONTENTS

PANEL 1 BLOODLINES	9
1. The book of life	11
2. Magic is everywhere	17
3. It was not a promising start	21
4. Schooldays	31
5. Brothers	37
6. Singing with the king	53
7. The quiet man	57
8. The passing of Friday 15 January, 2021	69
9. My life in a box	71
10. The letter	75
11. A visit to Mechelen	81

PANEL 2 FLIGHT OF THE CONDOR	87
1. In search of lost memories	89
2. Saudade	91
3. The Minas train	103
4. A Brazilian twist	109
5. Cinco cinco cinco	119
6. Festa junina	123
7. Uprooted	137

PANEL 3 CHASING THE ANCESTORS' BONES	141
1. Easy love	143
2. A romance	151
3. Meeting Aunt Spiridoula	161
4. A buskers' honeymoon	167
5. Zeco	181
6. Recycled genes	199
7. Bienvenue	203
8. Dancing with the bones	219

Madagascar Glossary	236

BLOODLINES

1
THE BOOK OF MY LIFE

THE BOOK OF MY LIFE HAS MANY PAGES MISSING. Some are frayed and furrowed with mould, others have suffered water damage, a washed-out cloud of ink dabbles. Letters and paragraphs have seeped out as through a colander while chapters I had torn out and shredded long ago are still there. I used to have boxes of objects too, memorabilia, cherished markers of my journey, precious treasures I thought would be with me forever, left behind in a life of wandering. An envelope of B&W photographs sent to me after my mother died is what remains of my parents and of my childhood. Memories of my early years, passengers on a ghost train speeding away from me across my horizon. And now I can hardly recall who I was as a child. It all happened in another lifetime it seems. Did it happen to someone else?

Lately a few sculptures, sent from Africa to my home town of Mechelen half a century ago, have travelled across a world of war zones, confusion and pollution to my quiet home at the rim of the Pacific Ocean, after many forgotten decades following the lives of my parents, my sister and her three growing boys from the shelves and cupboards of their homes in Belgium. A bearded fetish sitting on a stool, two blind concertina players carved from ebony, a naked shaman, emaciated, his ribs showing, his teeth grinning from a protruding chin, his hand grasping his wooden penis the size of his upper leg, witnessed the lives of my family during all my years of absence. I wish I could talk to them now, but the shaman only grins from behind the glass door of the wall-to-wall Ikea library that holds my growing comic and graphic novel collection. The much revered ninth art, as we call it where I come from. It started with a few Tintin books, in an attempt to recapture my lost childhood, and is now growing on steroids.

On one of my musical tours with my band, the Hottentots, I sent a box of old records home, stored forever in my brother's attic, rarities now from a bygone era. Narciso Yepes, Joao Gilberto, Jacques Brel, John Lee Hooker, Ravi Shankar, Chuck Berry, Bert Jansch, the Golden Gate quartet, Laurindo Almeida, Brownie McGhee, Cannonball Adderley, Martin Carthy, Baden Powell, Big Bill Broonzy—all gems from a pharaoh's crypt. My brother could not part with my Bob Dylan and Joni Mitchell albums, but that I can easily understand. I listen to the short-wave crackle of the vinyl grooves spinning all those nights ago on the second-floor bedroom of my teenage years and try to remember. And then, at the bottom of my cupboard, there lies a box of letters, unopened for years, that I have planned to burn. When aging, it is important to lessen our imprint on the world, decrease, as not to burden our loved ones with the weight of unwanted things. But I am taking my time to light the fire. Am I afraid to meet my former self? Would I rather let my past be?

I often think of my father, but fear that the fantasy image is more real than the man I never knew intimately. Our roles and our age difference got in the way. He was a devout Catholic, prayed before and after dinner and made the sign of the cross on his four children's brows when we kissed him goodnight. He was lucky to die before the worldwide paedophile scandal in the church burst like spoiled fruit crawling with maggots. His oldest son leaving the faith was a blow to him. He disapproved of my musical and my wandering ways too. I left as a young adult and did not return for many years, sucked into the vortex of the sixties and the magnitude and mysteries of the world, propelled by the volcanic eruptions that marked my destiny, ever a stranger in a strange land, the old familiarities bleached out like bloodstains in a bed sheet. People dear to me and revered objects vanished as I followed my path through one labyrinth after another of taboos, proprieties and beliefs, creating and re-creating myself with the puzzles of histories, codes and creeds, clutching temporary talismans and shedding used skins.

Over time I have framed some few recollections of my father and hung them in the salon of my heart, mythic fragments of my own Rosetta stone. My museum. Come and see me do my homework at the dining table beside my dad who is writing his judgements for the court. The room is dark as the winter night descends early. The green lampshade above us throws a beam of light on our silent concentration. And there we are, dad and I, in adjoining beds, interned together in a hospital, both with intestinal problems, not really talking much, but reading from our separate pile of books on our bedside tables. See the framed poster of the one film we saw together: Alfred Hitchcock's *North by North West*. I still think my father resembles Cary Grant. And, though we shared few intimate moments, I too look like him. My cousin Luc wrote me of his astonishment when he saw a recent photo of me, mistaking me for my dad. Luc is the other one in my family who shares my lifelong dedication and passion for music, and we both scaled rock walls and waded through murky moats to follow the piper. His love is for western classical music, mine is promiscuous and all over the place. His teenage self worshipped Mario Lanza. I shivered to Little Richard, Lebanese oud players and Big Bill Broonzy. He wrote me a letter recently:

'It comes down to this: you the road builder, I the nest-keeper. You the curious, the explorer, and ultimately the Ahasverus, the wanderer who walks the path of global renewal, while our grandfather taught me to become a conservative explorer of the past. Two different roads within the same domain.'

2

MAGIC IS EVERYWHERE

'Koe-eeel! Koe-eeel!'

An eastern koel has been calling me in my sleep until I finally wake up, startled into another day. A shower, breakfast of red papaya, blueberries, vanilla yoghurt and bircher muesli and off to my desk with a cup of coffee to check mail, news and social media, soon diverted and waylaid by the screen until, in what was once called 'the real world', an impressive, but harmless, huntsman spider runs down my chair, jumps on my foot to vanish behind the guitar rack. As I step out the backdoor a young blue-tongued lizard scurries beneath the well-worn grey leather sofa—the one a neighbour threw out and Parissa and I carried down the street. It is bright in the real word. The sun is out in force after a night of drenching rains. The grass is glistening. The sky ablaze. A magpie-lark perches on the table, scanning me doing the downward dog pose. A scream of black and white, like a chess board in a riot of green foliage shimmering behind him. Peewees, we call them here. It is the same bird that nearly caused me to lose an eye a few months ago. He has a mate and three squeaking brats. We share this veranda, our garden, neighbourhood, the coastal forests and swamps that separate us from the Pacific Ocean. But let me introduce you to some of the other traditional owners, that were here before me, and are still here. On the land, in the ocean and the sky.

The male bush turkey steps back a little, eyeballs me warily as I fill the watering can. He is in full regalia, dressed for a parade, strutting with the attitude of an LGBT Aztec temple priest. Bald, blood-red head and neck, deep yellow flaps, black plumage and fantail feathers—the colours of my home-town soccer team—and those of the Belgian flag. He grunts softly at me, his yellow wattle hanging low. It is breeding time and, as every year, he has been tirelessly scraping my carefully spread garden mulch to add to his growing mound. He has no off-switch, the Jack Russell Terrier of the feathered kingdom. Always on the go scraping my mulch and chasing other males clambering over our roof and out into the street. He builds; the girls come and visit him to mate and to lay their eggs in his towering incubator. He is partly responsible for the explosion of turkeys in our suburb and is still in his handsome prime. The turkey has his mound in the neighbour's backyard, after many attempts of establishing one over here. Our relationship goes back a while and would make a fine TV series. It has passion, dignity, respect, deeply ingrained behavioural patterns and a sense of the inevitable. It also has been tempestuous at times—like in the Jacques Brel song I have been singing again lately 'La Chanson des Vieux Amants '(The Song of Old Lovers).

'And each piece of furniture (in our case: trees, bushes & shrubs) Remembers the bursts of old storms'

The gales of recent days—the southern tail end of a Queensland tropical cyclone—have caused branches and palm fronds to drop everywhere. I drag them to the mountainous snake nest of green litter that my neighbour Phil and I share, and am soon crawling with ants—the big black ones. They're fine. The mini-ants are the cause of all the welts on my body. As I strip naked and brush off the crawlers, a flock of black cockatoos caw-caw from the forest canopy on the other side of the railway tracks like drunken studs in a strip joint. I linger a while with the currawongs and rainbow lorikeets chattering in the leafage above me, pull some weeds and unwanted growths, procrastinate studying the treetops and the moving herd of cloud sheep in the blue yonder, unwillingly frighten a dragon lizard and head inside to start writing about yesteryear. Digging up memories, finding my roots hidden below the ashes and the litter of the past. But first, dear friends, I welcome you from this fine day here in the Bay. Magic is everywhere whether we see it or not. I sometimes forget it too.

Please let me tell you my story.

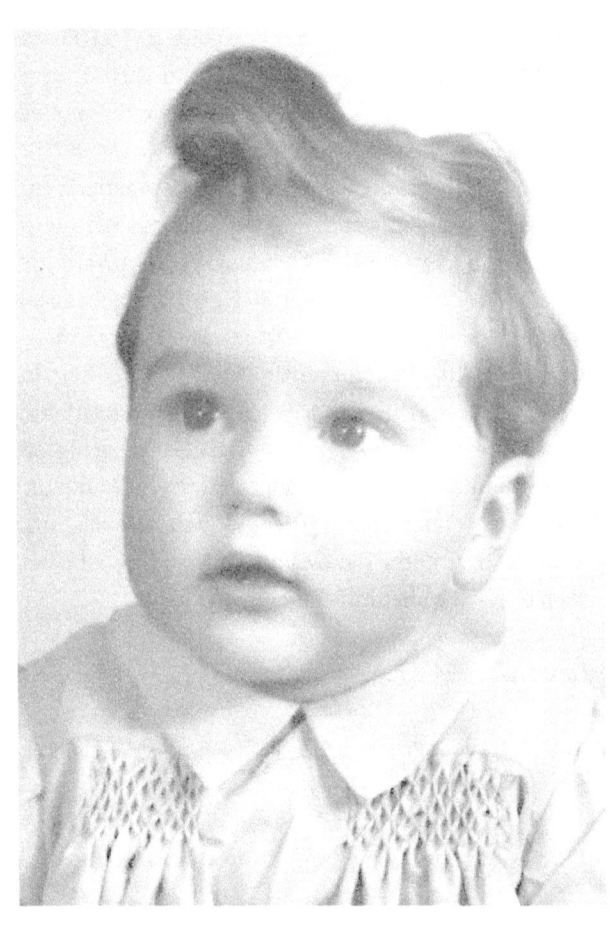

3

IT WAS NOT A PROMISING START

It was not a promising start. Two days before my birth on the 15th of April 1943 the allied forces commenced shelling. Three heavy bombardments destroyed hundreds of houses on the 19th, the day I was baptised. The sky was shattered with exploding bombs, turning the night clear as day and an indescribable panic gripped the Flemish town of Mechelen. The morgue was filled with corpses. My parents were living in a rented place in the Leopoldstraat. The Nazi occupation force had commandeered their home, cut holes through the walls to join it with two neighbouring houses, and made it their administrative headquarters. A year and a half later the first allied tanks rolled into town. The mayor who colluded with the Germans fled to South America and mobs turned on the collaborators. The onslaught of missiles diminished and stopped. The Nazis had fled. The victorious British army was now garrisoned there. Among the first faded photos taken of me in the backyard of our rented home, I look up from a zinc bathtub, two English soldiers behind me, smiling at the camera, cigarettes in their hands. Many years later—long after the end of hostilities—my younger brother Eric and I still cycled to school through neighbourhoods of burned-out shells, gaping holes, bombed craters where houses once stood, silent reminders of the madness. Perhaps not all memories can be sealed in a cage. As a boy, I suffered a recurring nightmare in which I was a partisan fighting off an invading army from the flat roof above the attic, acutely aware that I was fighting a losing battle. I always presumed these dreams to be figments of my lively imagination but now I am not so sure. My parents never told me these stories. A distant cousin only informed me of these facts last week, long after they had died. Memories locked up in a trunk and buried.

I was an infant then, but Mechelen already had a history. Settled in the Roman era, inhabited by Germanic tribes, converted to Christianity, ruled by the Dukes of Brabant and Burgundy, burned and sacked by the Spanish, plundered by French revolutionaries and German mercenaries, occupied by Napoleon, twice invaded in the 20th century by the Germans, formerly part of Holland, Mechelen has, since 1830, become incorporated into the new nation of Belgium. Belgium was an artificial state, devised by the surrounding great powers to prevent them from fighting yet another bloody war over the territory. A German king was imported to rule over us. Our town had seen it all. In past centuries the Mechlinians had endured outbreaks of the plague and cholera, experienced floods and witnessed heretics and witches burned at the stake or decapitated in the town square. For a short spell during the early 16th century, our little town had its fifteen years of fame as the regional capital of the Habsburg empire when the governess Margaret of Austria, a woman with attitude, a musician and a poet, held the reins of the Lowlands, one of the richest territories in Europe, in the name of the infant Charles V. Renaissance painters, polyphonic composers, printmakers and woodcarvers flourished. It was our moment of glory. But one night in 1546, a lightning strike blew up forty thousand kilos of dynamite, destroying a large section of the town and Margaret of Austria moved her court to Brussels. Her statue still graces the centre of Mechelen.

I was fortunate to be raised by kind-hearted parents, free from strife, in a continent rising from the rubble. My mother, Rita, was a sensitive woman, easily brought to tears. Petite but long-legged, with a slender neck, aquiline nose, blue eyes, eyebrows like the wings of a gliding heron, luscious blonde locks tied above her head—I never realized how attractive she was until I saw the photographs of her youth after she passed away. She was a dutiful woman, with a wicked sense of irony she held back like a rider holds a mare. For most of my childhood a maid lived with us to help with the chores of a large house and a family of four children—of which I am the oldest—but it was my mother who ran the household, cooked, did the shopping and made sure that we followed the dress and the code of manners expected of the children of a prominent man in a traditional town.

'Your father will be displeased if he hears that you…', was the stick she tried on us, though I knew my dad to be a softy.

I was fond of my mother but judged her weak to be hiding her power behind my dad—a reluctant sergeant himself. For most of us, our parents are better appreciated and understood once we have learned to stand on our own two feet. My mother was meant to be a queen in this traditional patriarchal family—not a king.

The king was my father, Albert, a judge in the town of Mechelen. It was in Margaret of Austria's 16th century palace that he handed out justice in his dramatic black robe and bonnet. It impressed me as a boy that policemen saluted my dad when he drove past an intersection in our town. To me, he looked like a movie star. Cary Grant. Humphrey Bogart. Tony Curtis. Errol Flynn. A receding hairline brushed back and smoothed into a shimmer with a dab of brilliantine pomade. Not a hair out of place. Polished leather shoes. Neatly-pressed pants. Ironed cotton shirts and handkerchiefs. V-line cardigans. Well-cut suits. But, a dandy he was not. Albert was a spiritual man, a devout Catholic. He almost enrolled in the seminary for the priesthood. It is thanks to his change of heart that I am writing these words. A romantic he was, looking at you with chestnut eyes, a warm smile that opened like an accordion, suddenly rising from the dining table to recite a poem. At wedding feasts, he might get up and—with a little prompting—burst into a bawdy song in the local dialect. How often did he lay his hand on my mother's hand at dinner time? My mother and father loved each other deeply and, even in their last years of life—when my dad was ill and they were sleeping in single beds—they held hands across the dividing space. Two younger brothers, a sister and I enjoyed a happy family life. We were an affectionate family and I adored and worshipped my dad. His heart was tender; his soul generous and fair. He was also blessed with the gift of music and could play along to the radio on our piano, by ear. It came therefore as a surprise that it was music that would create a major friction between us.

My Uncle Fernand owned a record shop in the Onze Lieve Vrouw straat. I was drawn to it, like a safety pin to a magnet. Most days, on my way home from school, I would pester him to track down obscure records that I could hardly afford to buy. When there were no customers we hung about the office at the back of the shop. It was his home away from home. Fernand shared the upstairs floors with six females: his wife—my cherished Aunt Lorette— four daughters, and a maid who was an adopted family member. I loved them all. I guess it was my home away from home. With these cousins, Eric and I swam in the Leuven canal, skated on the frozen lakes in the Vrijbroek Park, raced our bicycles to nearby villages, played hide and seek in the concrete war bunkers that dotted the countryside, and learned to dance. One cold winter night, hanging out in the shed at the back of the shop, an old guitar that hung on the wall took my fancy. The girls lent it to me permanently. I took it to bed that night, put my ear beside the sound hole and caressed the strings and, like in the song, my heart went ZING. I had found the key to the kingdom. The guitar remained beside my bed and guitars became my faithful companions for the rest of my life.

Flanders is a place of cold and rainy winters, grey and cloudy autumns and a spring that, in those times, always arrived late. Much of our youth was spent indoors. Paintings hung from every wall and corridor in our three-storey house—but for the bathroom, kitchen, the attic and the cheerless cellar. The cellar was where I sat in the dark if I did not eat all the meat on my plate; where I carried the pot of soup after meals in pre-fridge days; and where my brother and I raided my dad's wine collection. There were charcoal drawings of my grandparents in my father's office and a large canvas in a gilded frame by Alexander Wijnants of an elephant carrying a child on its back that overlooked the family meals for most of our childhood. A painter named Victor Quienen lived with us when we were young. I don't remember him but his portraits of my parents, the children and the maid were everywhere—even stored in the attic. Quienen became a well-known artist who went on to paint Edith Piaf and the Belgian king and queen. But there is one painting of his that I can see—after all those years—with my eyes closed. It shows a young girl from the Russian steppe: Dinska Bronska. My father used to recite the poem by Karel van den Oever that inspired the painting. The portrait had a spell on me—Dinska sitting by the window of the Lapland hotel, struggling to write a farewell letter to her parents, a blot of ink on the ten-cent paper she bought in the grocery store across the street. From a Prussian-blue scarf her flaxen hair has fallen on her reddened cheeks. She sucks on her pen. A smudge of tears runs from her eyes, blue as fjords, to the corner of her mouth. Dinska is waiting to board a rust-bucket steamboat to Canada. On the calendar of The Red Star Line she has admired the pictures of apples larger, and golden wheat higher, than in the camel-brown fields of Plocka. I was in awe of her courage. Fearful for her too. She was a dreamer on the brink of the unknown. I fancied going with her. I have always wondered what became of Dinska Bronska.

Paintings looked down from up high, but—for a child—the book shelves were easier to reach. And there were many books in the house, shelves in unexpected places, age-old volumes in a built-in cupboard. I usually read several at once, solving crimes with Sherlock Holmes and Hercule Poirot, laughing out loud with P.G. Woodhouse, scaring myself in bed with a macabre tale of Edgar Allan Poe or H.P. Lovecraft, then dreaming of being buried alive or fleeing from a killer gorilla. The calamitous narrative and the mysterious fate of Arthur Gordon Pym, who vanished in a rain of ashes and a shroud of mist left me forever wondering. I swapped Tintin for Steinbeck, the Odyssey which I read in ancient Greek at school for Alexander Dumas and Jules Verne at home, borrowed *Lord of the Flies* and *Animal Farm* from the Municipal Library around the corner of our house, stumbled into the *Heart of darkness*' and *All is quiet on the western front*, which my dad told me not to read. My bedroom became my time capsule, my portkey, a blue police box that took me below the sea, into the center of the earth and beyond the Milky Way, where I battled Martians and Triffids—sometimes until my mother came knocking at the door: 'Carl! Wake up! It is time for school.'

At lunch break and after school, priests from the Catholic college chaperoned us, in rows of three, to drop-off points nearest our homes. It was a chance to spin yarns of action and adventure for my best friends. Heroes travelled through outer space and back in time while we were led like sheep past the 14th century City Hall where I would marry years later. Galleons sank and human sacrifices were offered while us boys marched beside the 16th century tavern, De Kraan (The Tap), and around the city square. We thought nothing of riding wild stallions across the prairie while waiting for the order to cross the street beside the Post Office, in the shadow of the gothic Sint Rombouts cathedral that towers over the town at ninety-seven meters high. It was the cathedral that had given the inhabitants of the town the mock name 'Maneblussers' (moon extinguishers) when in the year 1687 the Mechlinians rushed to extinguish a fire in the tower, where the gothic windows had reflected the flaring of only the moon between clouds. Continuing along the Ijzerenleen, where my grandparents had a grocery store among shops with elegant facades from the 17th, 18th and 19th centuries, past the fish market where my great-grandfather was a merchant until he left his family for Paris to follow a musical dream, a woman or both, the chattering boys now crossed the Hoogbrug, the bridge across the river Dijle where my Aunty Malvina lived in an ancient tiny flat with leaning floors that looked out over the Lamot brewery with its rancid smell of hops. At the corner of the Onze Lieve Vrouw straat where the file of kids disbanded, the stories always ended in a cliffhanger. To be continued. In Mechelen I tramped on the bones of my ancestors and strayed through the centuries each day, skipping from the gothic into the baroque, the renaissance, rococo and neo-classicism while, inside my head, gladiators and pirates were a preoccupation sending me off in a spaceship to somewhere else. It was my escape valve from a regimented school life.

4
SCHOOL DAYS

I DON'T OWE ANY ALLEGIANCE TO A PARTICULAR DEITY these days, but was however brought up as a good Catholic boy, attending kindergarten with the nuns, the all-boys primary as well as high school under the rule of priests. Born with a devil's hand, the Holy Sisters of the Sacred Chastity Belt hit me on the left hand as soon as I picked up a pencil; and that was only the entrée. Even Leuven University where I studied law was a Catholic institution.

Rombout was my best friend at high school. To avoid failing my exams during the years I became distracted by music, Bo tutored me in math through many a hot summer night. When I heard about the stuffed animals, gathering dust in the attics of the college, it was my friend who sneaked up there under cover of darkness, so that I could enhance my bedroom with a mounted civet cat and a dog-shark with teeth-like needles. My cousin Paul gained a kangaroo with straw creeping from its pouch. At college, straight-faced Rombout, was regarded as a good angel, who sang in the school choir and was well-behaved, while God's representatives on earth had cast me into the murky realms of purgatory. The school prefect foretold that my prospects were bleak. How that college has changed with the times! The last time I passed by that school at leaving time, students were smoking a joint and kissing girls at the school gate. I sure missed out. But back in the early sixties it was still a mediaeval institution. Almost all our teachers were priests, many of them frustrated men from the rural areas. Had they realized, as late teenagers, what a vow of celibacy and strict obedience to the church and its rules for the rest of their lives really meant? The fact that most priests lived inside the college gave the buildings a monastic aura. Discipline was tight. And that is an understatement.

After school, between 4.45 and 7pm, the school rules forbade us to be out on the streets. We were meant to be at home, doing homework and study. Priests on bikes patrolled the town to catch stragglers. Students were not allowed to enter a cinema or café unless accompanied by their parents. The Catholic college had its own cinema on Sunday afternoons—my brother Eric and I were regular goers. My music education was limited to Gregorian chants in the school's assembly hall. Each year I was selected for the school choir, but my parents kindly arranged a doctor's certificate that absolved me from attending the 7am spiritual vocal workout at school. Then there was the interesting concept of confession, where us boys entered a dark box each week to inform one of our teacher-priests of the dirty thoughts we'd been having. Creepy. Any contact with girls from the Catholic girl school, of course, was seriously frowned upon. When my Aunt Lorette allowed her daughters to invite Eric and I, and a few school friends, to a little birthday party at her home, the news somehow

reached the director. Squeezing my arm with a trembling wrist, the saintly little man in his purple robe accused me of immoral behaviour.
— 'Immoral behaviour?' I was puzzled.
He gave me another nasty squeeze, his face close to mine and hissed:
— 'There has been dancing!'
I did not know of any of the Ten Commandments, brought down by Moses from the mountain where God lives, that proclaimed 'Thou shall not dance!' but this was not the moment to score a point of dogma. In any case, by then I had switched on to a different channel when Jerry Lee Lewis, Howling Wolf and Ray Charles thundered into my second-floor coloseum on gilded chariots, pulled by winged stallions sweating ebony and spewing fire, leaving scorch marks on the roll-top desk inherited from my grandfather. I was already a lost cause.

I confess that I hadn't taken to this kind of policing, and did my very best to put spanners in the educational wheels. I made fake phone calls to the director, under the guise of a student's parent, to complain about the behavior of a brutal priest. Posing as a man from the funeral parlour, I called the director to inform him that a hearse would shortly arrive to collect the corpse of an unpopular priest, who supposedly had died from a stroke in his room. This incident caused quite an upheaval in the school. Sadly, someone gave the game away and I was dismissed for three days. Soon after I was caught distributing an obscene epic, of my own hand, that had the saintly man in purple as its raunchy hero. But the little bastard took revenge. He summoned my mother to school and read out the dirty bits to my blushing mum, who came home outraged—not angry with me, but with whom she called 'that perverted man' who had so embarrassed her. I was dismissed for another three days. On a spiritual retreat where all the boys were strongly reminded that the priesthood was the best professional option for their future, I put a dead rat in the bed of the head honcho. After boasting about it to my friends the news reached the priest, a tall aristocratic man who also wore a purple sash over his frayed black soutane, a chain smoker of cigars, who stank like an ashtray, we nicknamed 'Dirty Edward'. I had to resort to a sudden overpowering interest in the priesthood to save my arse and avoid being expelled from school. It just worked. When in our last year of high school all my classmates, corralled by priests, went on a guided tour of the ancient and Catholic architectural wonders of Rome, my buddy Bo and I hitchhiked to Frankfurt to explore the jazz clubs. We had a great time, even though no jazz club allowed these underage boys in. On our return my arm was squeezed repeatedly by the trembling wrist. I managed to get out of the Sint Rombouts college with the skin of my teeth. They still send me requests for financial contributions and invitations to their class reunions, but my rocket ship left that planet a long time ago.

5
BROTHERS

IT WAS A COLD NIGHT. THE FULL MOON WAS HALOED, the branches of the gum trees and the Poinciana tree in the garden creaking and swaying in the gale, the king tides ominously crashing and rumbling in the ocean beyond. Snuggled in bed with the electric blanket on, I lay, propped up by pillows, with a gem of a comic book by Edmond Baudoin, one of my favourite French graphic novelists. *Piero'* is the title of the book and it is the name of Edmond's older brother. The boys grew up, constantly drawing together, sketching their fantasies and games on paper, copying images from post office calendars and newspapers, practicing horse's hooves and, later on, girls, astonished to discover, when they first went to school, that not everyone else drew. Boys would barter marbles for a drawing of the map of France; girls traded a kiss for a sketch of James Dean. It was Piero, the older brother, who was chosen to enrol in art school, while Edmond would have the serious profession of an accountant. Yet Piero dropped out, disillusioned, and it was Edmond who persisted to become a much-loved author, first published at age 40. Not unlike Robert Crumb, another cartoonist idolising his talented older brother Charles, who abandoned art while Robert became the well-known artist. I fell asleep dreaming of comics and brothers.

The next morning a headline in The Guardian grabbed me with a quote by Noel Gallagher of the band Oasis: 'I liked my mum until she gave birth to Liam'. After reading the affectionate tale of Edmond and Piero last night, I was shocked at first, then recalled my cousins, who could not stand one another at all when young, relentlessly taunting and mocking each other. Chalk and cheese. Opposite characters. Cain and Abel. The unique stories of siblings would require a separate branch of literature—like science fiction or detective stories—and have been a steady theme for the movies. Who can ever forget Marlon Brando and Richard Davalos in Elia Kazan's *East of Eden*; Rod Steiger and Marlon Brando in *On the Waterfront*; Alain Delon and Renato Salvatore in Luchino Visconti's epic saga *Rocco and his brothers*. Blood brothers, growing together or growing apart. Tales of love, loss, jealousy, rivalry, conflict, lifelong friendships, enmity and the dissolution of blood ties.

One of my earliest, vivid memories is of my mother sitting by the dining room window looking out in to the Langenieuwsstraat on a grey afternoon. Across the street two neighbourhood pubs stood side by side: De Vroege Morgend (the early morning) and De Laten Avond (the late evening); a family grocery store on the corner and a bakery down the street. These are long gone now. It was shortly after the war and well before the age of supermarkets. I was sitting on my mum's lap and made a sneaky lunge for her breast, only to be rebuffed.

— 'You are too old for that now Kamanneke!'.

These breasts now served my brother Eric, two years younger than me. Soon he would share the bed with me in the room on the first floor, and become my best buddy and playmate throughout my childhood. Together we would dream up a fantasy universe of our own, not unlike Piero and Edmond.

My parents were devout Catholics but my first idol was not Jesus, but Tintin, or Kuifje as he is named in my native Flemish. 'Kuif' means quiff or forelock. The Weekly Franco-Belgian comics magazine first appeared in 1946. I was three years old and there is a photo of me, posing in an angelic blue top with a frilly white collar, my hair brushed into a wave, a cat-gets-the-fish smile and the colourful mag before me.

Subtitled "The Magazine for the Youth from 7 to 77", it was to become my bible and weekly addiction. Several ongoing stories unfolded with one or two pages weekly, ending on cliff-hangers that left an impatient generation of Belgian and French kids waiting eagerly for the next issue. It featured all our heroes. Besides Tintin the travelling reporter, Captain Haddock and all the unforgettable characters created by Herge, there was Corentin, a Breton orphan who flees the house of his uncle, an abusive drunkard, runs off to sea to be shipwrecked, leading to a remarkable odyssey in 18th century India and China. Paul Cuvelier, its creator, then brought, at the request of Herge, his hero back as the grandson of the original, for Corentin's exploits in the Wild West, one of my all-time favourite comics, its allure augmented by the fact that it was out of print for many years.

Turn the page of the weekly and you'd meet the very British, Professor Philip Mortimer, a bearded, pipe-smoking scientist, with his friend Captain Francis Blake of MI5 and their nemesis Colonel Olrik. They make their appearance at the start of a global war provoked by an Asian superpower (it was published just after WWII), in a riveting drama set in central Asia that runs over 3 books. They go on to solve complex crimes and mysteries of espionage, will chance upon ancient secrets deep inside the Pyramids, voyage to the lost continent of Atlantis, into the Jurassic past and the distant future in a sabotaged time machine, a trap set by a vengeful scientist.

Just as much-loved were the books of Alex, drawn by Jacques Martin, another master of the *ligne claire style*, besides Herge and Edgar Jacobs, the author of Blake and

Mortimer. Alex is a young Gallo-Roman in the late Roman republic, fearless and generous, originally a slave, but later adopted by a nobleman, contemporary to Julius Caesar. His adventures take him far and beyond the empire, to the Greek islands, north Africa, Mesopotamia, among the Gaulish tribes, as far as China. The artwork is fabulous and historically accurate. The series commenced in 1948 and continues today. Since Eric and I had to cram much ancient history and read the Greek and Roman works in the original language, Alex's adventures injected much-needed magic into the classes of dead languages, conjugations by rote and laborious translations at school. Compared to the British and American comics, which were discouraged by parents in these countries, and ranged from superheroes to ducks, rabbits and mice, the Franco-Belgian axis of the Ninth Art was defined by detailed art work, intricate plots and veracity, while providing a superb window into a wider world, exploring foreign cultures and history. Tintin, Corentin, Alex, Blake and Mortimer were role models for

---

FOOTNOTE: There was much more fun in the magazine of course, including some of the most recognisable Flemish comic book characters: Marc Sleen's anti-hero, Nero, bald, middle-aged, simple-minded and unemployed. He still writes letters to Santa and is intimidated by his genius son Adhemar. Nero is also immortal, features in an avant-garde opera and has statues in two Belgian towns. And then there are Suske and Wiske (in French: Bob et Bobette; in English: Spike and Suzy; Willy and Wanda in the US) by Willy Vandersteen. Suske is a dapper, smart, courageous lad, originally an orphan. His eternal companion, Wiske, is a strong-headed, inquisitive, stubborn and brave girl. Lambik, another bald middle-aged man with a huge ego, but a mostly noble soul where battles between his guardian angel and his demon are fought, provides comic relief. The rest of

my brother and I, setting our imagination and curiosity alight. My idols were all travellers.

Of course, every issue was kept and collected, though some of the early ones I cut up to glue as illustrations in the history album that chronicled the battles Eric and I fought with our toy soldiers. I have always repented that sacrilegious act. My dad made sure to have the 52 yearly issues bound later on, but just those few were missing. All four of us kids have read those volumes so many times that they must be embedded—plot, dialogue, drawings and colours—in the corridors and walls of our brains. Toy soldiers always seem to play a part in a boy's childhood. Our varied assortment of knights in armour, para commandos with machine guns, pistol-packing cowboys, Indians with tomahawks, gladiators with swords and shields, Africans with spears and bows, astronauts with laser guns were divided into battalions and faced off on the carpet in my dad's office. Sometimes school friends came to do battle

---

the cast includes Professor Barabas who invented the Gyronef, a prototype helicopter before these were a reality; the parental figure, Aunt Sidonia; and Jerommeke who was brought from prehistory by an alchemist, has x-ray vision and superhuman strength. I always presumed that these heroes were too quintessentially Flemish to captivate an international audience but the books have been translated in countless languages, including Latin, Chinese, Persian, Swahili, Icelandic, Tibetan and Gaelic. In Belgium, Nero, Suske, Wiske and Lambik are cultural icons, probably better known than the prime minister of the country. TV series, films, theatrical adaptions and statues have been dedicated to them. As of 2017, 339 albums of Suske and Wiske have been published. You can buy them at your local grocery store, a supermarket or newsagent.

with their own forces. Invaded, Eric and I turned allies. Our visiting enemies then acquired an officially named country on the fantasy maps I drew in our history book. I vaguely recall that my nation was named Karnakia, but I know for sure Eric's country was Bangweolo, foreshadowing his lifelong passion for Africa, and the Congo in particular.

Many a summer our parents shared the hire of a holiday home by the North Sea beaches or the French Mediterranean coast with the Van Roey family. Frieda was my age. Her younger sister Claire matched Eric. We were inseparable. The four of us, their sibling Patrick, my little sister Denise and a few other suicidal kids, keen for a thrill after digging too many holes in the sand and shoveling futile castles against the tide, crawled, each in turn, through drainpipes, traipsed on high walls or jumped the slippery boulders of the breakwaters at the end of the piers above the churning sea in a game dubbed 'Courage Challenges'. Eric was accident prone and, while I broke wrists or collarbone, his head was his weak spot. There were regular dramas with bumps, bruises and cuts, band-aids and bandages. Frieda was a tomboy and a keen booklover. I taught her how to piss upright against the wall. We once ran away to Holland together, until hunger turned us back. Together we devised our own version of the Tintin weekly, with original heroes, plots and illustrations. We named it Bobeson and distributed samples among our friends. I recall how laborious the copying and colouring by hand was. Like in the real magazine, every week the stories ended with the magic words: to be continued. To encourage Eric and my younger sister Denise to read more we selected 3 books per week, each inserting a bookmark to show how far advanced we were. I confess that, as the oldest, I was usually the instigator of these schemes.

Though I was never one to attend soccer matches as a child or as an adult, my father, Eric and my younger brother Luc supported the local team of K.V.Mechelen at each home match for most of their lives. Of course, everyone followed the World Cup soccer Games. Sports were ever present in a youth's life, but it was during the autumn and winter months that it galvanised our games. We played soccer in school and rode our bikes, but in the fallow the real action was indoors. From our bag of marbles we selected, according to colour, a dozen teams of 11 players each. A larger marble, often called the 'Shooter', served as soccer ball. Of course, there were rules, goal posts and a score board. Twelve competing countries: six for Eric, six for me, both of us knuckling down on the faded, threadbare carpet under the bare tiles of the attic, the chill winds blowing through the cracks between the walls and roof. Eric's favourite team consisted of large dark green marbles, representing, yet another premonition, the Congo.

The Tour de France was also a favourite sports event. For a month each year Eric and I returned from school to join my father glued to the radio for the incoming sprint. In those days the teams still represented their countries and not corporations. We had acquired some sixty plastic cyclists as birthday and Christmas presents and had named each one of them. We christened our version 'the Tour of the 7 Games' and, like the real contest, it took many days to complete. With the throw of a pair of dice each cyclist advanced across a series of board games, a gift from Saint Nicolas, spread out on my dad's—who preferred to work under the green lamp in the dining room—largely unused office desk. Frame by frame, the tour crawled like a caterpillar through the game of the goose, snakes and ladders, a car race, a horse race etc.The cyclists also left the board games to hit the floor, follow the patterns on the carpet at the behest of the dice and made excursions through the bedrooms and the hallway, now forwarded with a stretch of our arms, a stretch that was always a bit longer when our own favourites had their turn. As with the history book, the results of these soccer and cycling tournaments were diligently annotated in yearly ledgers.

But what caused most havoc in the house were the

regular epic car races, when all our toys would be shoved forward, starting in the cellar among the racks of wine bottles and heaps of coal, each car, metal, plastic or tin, four wheels, three or none, escalading stair by stair, through the hallway, the dining room and the kitchen, up to the first floor, the race working its way through every room to the second floor and all the way up to the attic, a process that could take a week. Meanwhile it was as if the place was mined—with toys. Cars left on the staircase, under the dining table, in the hall or in my dad's office, forgotten in unexpected passages, stranded in corners of the bedrooms, to the cries of alarm of my vexed mother. My parents were extremely tolerant when it came to our games.

Over the warmer months our activities moved outdoors. Eric and I cycled with cousins and friends all through the countryside, held real cycle races, played tennis and swam in the canal or the pools in Keerbergen or Hofstade. On boy scout camping trips in the forests of the Ardennes, we were taught how to build rafts and rope bridges, construct a decent bonfire and throw a quick, rough forest shelter together that we then slept in. We spied on deer, birds and boars, learned to identify the leaves of the native trees, the planets and constellations of the night sky, memorised sailor's knots and, after a run of camps and skill tests, we received totem names at initiation ceremonies around the campfire, just as we imagined happened among the Indian tribes. I became a cheerful squirrel. I probably would have preferred to be a panther like my friend Leo, but since then I have learned that I am more squirrel than panther. These ten days long jaunts in nature were the counterpoint to our games at home and have engendered my love of nature for the rest of my life.

My family never had a real wireless or record player at home, except for the one I acquired as a teenager. The only music in our house, besides the occasional piano piece from my dad, was a radio distribution network with four channels that brought us programs from the Belgian national radio—one in Flemish, the other in French—interspersed with emissions from the BBC or the Dutch broadcasting service in Hilversum. A dial from 1 to 4 clicked us into different options. My brother Eric and I shared a double bed in the room adjoining my parents' bedroom. 'Playing radio' was our bedtime game. In these nightly entertainments we imitated the downstairs distribution system. By calling out numbers Eric switched the imaginary dial and I would provide the content. This started out me singing songs I had heard on the radio and in the music shop of my Uncle Fernand, with my brother retaining the power to change the station, if my song didn't please him. There were also channels where stories were in constant progress and Eric could channel surf to follow the adventures of his favourite heroes, each with the nightly ending 'to be continued', as in the Tintin magazine. Over the years our radio world expanded with a parade of vampires, vikings, robots, pirates, cannibals, ghosts, inventions, magic potions. Stations became interactive, allowing my brother to gain personal friends and gather allies with whom he could converse and strike deals, participate in the action and influence events. I provided a range of voices and sound effects. Eric corresponded with these fictional characters by putting letters in the drawer of my bedside table and I would slip replies and regular newsletters, detailing the latest happenings in our radio universe, in his.

And then my brother went to boarding school. It happened suddenly. A priest at college manhandled my little brother so roughly that clumps of his hair were pulled from their roots. I was incensed; Eric was traumatised. Together, we confronted our father with an ultimatum.
— 'We refuse go to school unless you complain to the director!'
And complain he did, threatening to report the priest to the police. As one of the town's judges this must have made an impact. But Eric could not face returning to the scene of his torturer and chose to move into a boarding school of Christian brothers. I never knew whether he considered his removal a blessing or a punishment. Perhaps a bit of both. Eric always held his cards close to his chest. He was an enigma hidden behind a jest. A twist of fate had shifted both our lives. I lost my playmate, my potato-headed brother with the twinkling blue eyes, cheeks that dimpled with each smile. We were close as thieves. The games we invented, the imaginary worlds we inhabited, it all came to an end like the closing of the curtain, the slamming of the gate, the felling of a tree. The nightly radio games Eric and I played were replaced with a real radio that I built inside my grandfather's cigar box to listen to Buddy Holly and Chuck Berry cracking, oscillating in and out of range from Luxembourg, huddled beneath the blankets as not to wake my parents in the room next door. I was almost fourteen and had the

room to myself.

When Eric left boarding school, I was already lodging in the university town of Leuven. Two years later, we shared a room, both of us law students now, but our paths had diverged. I still remember the symbolic parting, leaving our parents' house, ready for a Friday night out on the town in Mechelen. We walked together to the street corner of the Louisastraat and the One-Lieve-Vrouwstraat, where the Gothic Church of Our Lady across the river Dijle branched our path.

— 'Do you want to come with me to the Harten Aas?'
— 'Do you want to join me and my friends at the Bowling Club?'

Something in me hoped, but I knew we wouldn't. I stepped left towards de Harten Aas, where musicians, painters, travellers and hippies converged. Eric went right to the Bowling Club where the young lawyers in suits and lads-about town congregated.

After my studies I left the country, first for Africa, then travelling east. When my brother received his degree, he chose to teach in the newly independent Democratic Republic of the Congo instead of doing obligatory service in the army. He stayed four years in Africa and never stopped talking about it. 'The best years of my life' he called them. Franco and the OK Jazz band became the nostalgic soundtrack to his memories, while Fats Domino remained the leitmotif of his teenage years. Whenever we met in later years our sense of humour was the link that survived our childhood closeness. Eric was a gentleman with a soft heart. I can't recall a single fight during all the years, but for his complaint to Luc, my younger brother, that I threw one of his cyclists that threatened my own favourite, in the stove. I have no memory of this, but Eric had, and I must, belatedly, apologise. He died, but when I am alone at home I still talk to him aloud, cracking jokes in our native dialect, our secret code.

6
SINGING WITH THE KING

A VIRUS HAD DESCENDED FROM MY THROAT INTO MY chest, then climbed into my head and vivid dreams accompanied a rough night of sniffing, snooting and coughing. The most memorable dream arrived just before waking.

Thunder claps rolled boulders across the heavenly bowling alley high above me. Golden veins of lightning broke the starless firmament in random pieces and I suddenly thought of the Berlin conference of 1884, when the colonial masters carved up the African continent in a scramble to lay their eggs in the nests of other birds. In Otto von Bismarck's residence on Wilhelmstrasse, Otto, the explorer Stanley, the notorious king of Belgium, Leopold II, and others drew lines on incomplete maps, thus splitting ancient African tribes and laying the foundations of the tragic divisions that still plague the continent a century and a half later, all in a conqueror's rapacity for ivory, gold, rubber, timber and a work force. The Great Plunder.

The next salvo of God's cannons unleashed a downpour. I hurried to the nearest doorway and found myself in a hotel in a foreign country where I would meet, for the first time, Baudouin or Bodewijn as he is called in Flemish, king of the

Belgians during my younger years when I still resided there. Baudouin was a shy, nerdy, and a deeply spiritual man, a Catholic of much graciousness and modesty, loved by all, his occasional faux pas forgiven—such as praising his grandfather, Leopold II, the mass-murderer of the Congo, in a speech on Congolese Independence Day before the assembled dignitaries and elected representatives of the brand-new nation state. Baudouin had been reluctant to become king, wishing instead to be a priest, but the circumstances of the abdication of his father catapulted him into the job. He always stood by his pious principles to the point of refusing to sign the law permitting abortion. In the typical roundabout Belgian manner of resolving tricky political issues, the parliament then suspended his powers for one day so that the law could be passed, reinstating his powers on the next day. King Baudoin married Fabiola, a Spanish princess and another staunch Catholic , but the couple was unable to have children. Was that why he was often called 'the sad king'?

I knew someone who knew someone who had been picked up by the king in his convertible sports car and as a student, hitching rides to the university town of Leuven, I fancied that, perhaps one day, I too would get a ride with the king. And now Baudouin himself stepped down the stairs in my hotel with two minders to join me in the foyer. We had a polite, friendly and forgettable conversation about Belgian history and then he left. I was thrilled, gushing to my wife Parissa, who is as often in my dreams as she is in real life, explaining who he was when the king returned with five other men and joined me at the dining table.

We were sitting side by side, slurping chervil soup, white napkins at our throats. Waiters served shrimp croquettes with a dash of deep-fried parsley as the conversation turned to music. He confessed that he had always wanted to play an instrument and sing, but that the responsibilities of his position had not made it possible. He spoke to me in a heavily accented Flemish, as was his manner. A king speaking Flemish was still a novelty then. In the days of my grandfather Flemish was banned in schools as the language of education. For generations the royal family had spoken French, long the parlance of the ruling class and the bourgeoisie Bruxellois, though they descended from the same German stock as the British and other European monarchs. I pulled a songbook out of my pocket and found a wordy song with a catchy refrain. I presumed it was some pop tune of the 1950s, but if it was I had never heard it before. Together the king and I sang, our arms measuring the beat. In the pauses his companions attempted to interrupt—mostly to discuss the etymology of the words— till we took up singing once again. We both chuckled at our mistakes and ventured harmonies. Bodewijn was the embodiment of kindness and culture, the friend I had always wanted. I was deeply moved and wept in my dream. And then he left to climb the stairs, his entourage in tow, and disappeared from view.

I wanted to tell him so much more. I wanted to tell him that I had a lovely wife who is a great singing teacher and was sure that she would be happy to come to his palace at no charge to sing with him. I resolved to write him a letter. Perhaps I should send him my book *Tarab*, but dismissed that idea, fearing that the accounts of my drug experiments might put him off. But the enchanting dream touched my heart and when I recounted it to Parissa at the breakfast table, I broke into tears again.

— 'That king is you', she said.

Or could it have been my dad?

7
THE QUIET MAN

A FEW YEARS AGO I received a photocopy of a family tree, researched by a distant relative. It stretches four centuries into the past, but only follows the artery of my father's blood. If counting the bloodlines from both parents over twelve generations and four centuries, I would have a giant redwood tree of four thousand ancestors. But all I can see here are a few cones, labelled with names and dates of birth and death, hanging off a slender cypress tree. Besides the silent fragment of a map just a few second-hand whispers have reached me from the grapevine that is my birthland of Flanders. Rumour has it that the ancestral tree could not be traced further back, blocked by an unregistered forefather, possibly the illegitimate child of a priest or a nun. Considering my childhood, ruled and leg-ironed by priests and nuns, there must be some truth in this.

Another tale concerns an ancestor who became an officer in the British army to fight Napoleon in the battle of Waterloo and returned, strutting on horseback through the centre of Mechelen, in a victory parade. Whether these tales are true I do not know. I have never been able to communicate with the person that compiled this family history. Perhaps some mysteries are better left alone to become legends.

The earliest forefather I am aware of is my great-grandfather, Engelbert, born in 1860. I was given a chance to peer into his soul thanks to my granduncle, Albert Van Hoogenbemt, who wrote a book about his father, titled 'De Stille Man' or 'The Quiet Man'. It was awarded the Triennial State Prize for narrative prose in 1938. Albert was 13 years old when his father died and relied, besides his young memories, on the correspondence between his father and his patient, angel-like, mother Theresia. The book makes me a voyeur of the drama of their private lives.

The couple had a store with a warehouse at the Fish market of Mechelen and both were music lovers. The songs from Schumann's 'Dichterliebe' were their favourites. In the beginning of their marriage the evenings would often be spent around the piano. Engelbert's clavier would moan like a haunted soul, then rise triumphantly like a victorious army. 'He enters the source of the music' thought Albert, 'he plucks a flower from the darkness', as the boy lay in his childhood bed, eyes wide open, suspended in the silence between songs, waiting in anticipation for his mother's voice, that 'dark, warm voice like a fountain in the night'.

Engelbert was a man of culture, a large man with a pointy blond beard, a taciturn composer and a passionate perfectionist with a grand dream. Yet he was also a weak figure, a coward, a man of shadows who drank and fought in bars, spied and pestered young lovers. He was a tormented soul and—in what we would now call a mid-life crisis—abandoned his wife and children to flee Mechelen with another woman, for a life in Paris to try his luck in the classical music world of his time.

This was his goodbye note:

— 'I have gone to Paris with Lydia. Don't look for me. I'm not coming back anyway. The business is thriving enough to support you and the children. I am too weak of character to stay longer. That's all.'

Theresia was left to run the business and raise their seven children. She too was a musician, but had to let go of her studies. A story experienced by women all over the world. Her heartache and anguish are detailed in the many long letters sent to her sister after his leaving. These were the letters given to Albert, the writer, by an uncle many years after his father passed away. It left my granduncle shaken. His parents had always concealed these traumatic events from their children and the letters propelled him on a quest to unveil who his father really was. To read of Theresia's despair is harrowing. Her realisation of the loss and betrayal by her husband, the aspiring artist to whom she had dedicated her life and dreams, while she denied herself, rattled me. I have read the letters many times, recognising her turmoil. In my twenties I had received a very similar 'Don't look for me. I'm not coming back.' note. I identified with her attempts to comprehend what made him leave, seesawing between accusing and excusing him.

Engelbert's Parisian vision soon turned sour, the fantasy an illusion, the dream a nightmare. And the letters to his wife arrived steadily. Theresia copied them word for word in the correspondence with her sister, and now I am reading them here, over a century later.

— 'I knew that beauty existed, and I wanted my life to be my dream. But I have strived for something that was too far to achieve and so I have passed your love by.'

After so many years of marriage he finally vents to his wife the unspoken battles fought with himself. And we see the sulking, unhappy man, troubled by doubt, pacing the floor at home or escaping into a drunken night of self-loathing, the vain perfectionist who wanted to be like Beethoven or Schumann, who once composed sonatas and concertos, who had fled for years from his workroom, his piano untouched, while his wife tended to the shop and the children.

'Living dead' he labels himself, 'I lacked the passion that could have lifted me over my weakness and cowardice'.

Music had become a beautiful, but poisonous flower. The days of inspiration became fewer. The periods of depression increased. He was 48 now and Paris was his last chance to redeem himself. A new man, a new life, a new ambience and to finally compose, compose, compose. Lacking confidence to go it alone, he dragged Lydia, a cellist and a long-time friend, besotted with him, into his scheme. 'I chose my best friend as the victim', he writes and treats her cruelly when they go out at night, chatting up bar ladies in front of her to demean her. To make the break of his departure final, and blow up his bridges, he purposely creates a scandal by abandoning his wife and children. This too would boast his resolve.

Within two months Engelbert returned home to his forgiving wife and his children. He was the shell of the man. He rarely touched the keys of the clavier now, was often distracted and brooding. And soon he was ill and we hear their final farewell as he lies on his deathbed, his head on Theresia's shoulder.

— 'Only you have been true to me, with a love that never ebbed. Like a lesser treasure I left your love aside. Why? Because it was a given. I did not have to fight for it. I returned as a poor man and found your love as a lamp in the night. I see clear, now that it is too late.'

She kisses his forehead and wipes his tears. When he recalls the futility of his life and the destructive things he has done, she holds him.

— 'Come, let us forget in sleep Engelbert. All this is past.'

He remembers their first meeting after his concert. She was eighteen and dressed in white. When he offered his hand, she touched it with her fingertips. A few days later he visited her house and presented her with a breastpin, a coral hand, red as blood. She was worried at first since it was a strange gift, but accepted when he said that it came from Italy. He had built a little love and trampled it.

— 'Talk to me of the past, Engelbert! Why dig up all the misery, Why?'
— 'The beauty of life was too big for me… I couldn't… All is so beautiful…'

A sudden wind rattled the bedroom window and a lash of rain whipped the glass.

— 'How late is it?'
— 'I don't know Engelbert.'
— 'God, how long the night lasts!'
— 'Rest my love. Sleep softly'

He died at 53, before his grandson, my dad, was born. Theresia died at 89. I was four years old.

Albert, the poet and writer who is my father's namesake, the man who told me stories, sitting on his lap, in the backroom of my grandfather's grocery store, attempted in his book to discover who is father really was.

'I was rather young when father died. He has gone through my life like an autumn dream: quiet, strange, subdued, with sometimes heavy outbursts, a bit sad. I have always looked up to him in awe, and my love was as much worship as affection. As a child we see the things pertaining to our parents, beautiful and big; but later big things become small, and small things become big. So, when I became a man, I started seeing him smaller, a bit helpless. But now I have come to the years where the concept of father, which the human of flesh and blood keeps concealed from the child's eye, disappears and one confronts the man, to whom one does remain attached to with all one's being, but which one want to understand.'

The blood of both men, the passionate, but haunted, music lover and the inquisitive poet and writer, pulses in my veins, while my heart beats for the songstress of so much strength and deep emotion that was my great-grandmother, Theresia, always living for the happiness of others, ever helpful, busy, present without asking questions, never talking much about herself, hearing it all, sustaining it all, without demanding anything in return. At the end of his book Albert admits that we can never truly know the secret life of another. 'Few know their own self. Humans are such strange beings', he concludes. Yet, having heard their life stories and read their intimate letters I wonder whether I now know my great-grandfather better than my own father. Engelbert's letters allowed me to look in to afflicted recesses of his heart, while seeing the man who my dad really was remains a puzzle with too many pieces lost. After decades of absence and deep canyons of distance, with genuine faraway affection but limited communion, like messages found in bottles among the plastic garbage on the beaches of the oceans of the world, my dad morphed into a cardboard cut-out of a movie star outside the Palace Cinema. Perhaps the attitude of previous generations, when fathers did not reveal emotions or intimacies has changed in this 21st century, where parents are given permission to be friends with their offspring, though in most of the societies I have known, the father figure is still an authoritative figure deserving of respect and never questioned, his inner life concealed.

Albert's oldest brother, Louis or Lodewijk as he is called in Flemish, my grandfather, must have known Engelbert much better, but never talked to me about his dad, although I spent much time with grandpa and even slept with him as a twelve-year-old boy when he became a widower. I inherited Lodewijk for my middle name from him, while he inherited the love for music from Engelbert and Theresia. What goes around, comes around. In a corner of the quiet salon above his store a gramophone played scratchy shellac 78 records of opera and classical music, giving the salon an air of reverence. The heavy curtains dimmed the light, leaving all the space to the mysterious voices and orchestras that, to this young child, came from another planet in a distant past. My music loving cousin Luc, who worshipped Lodewijk, adopted his musical taste and remained faithful to it for ever after, though I have tried my best to seduce him with other mellifluous marvels. Grandpa left Luc his record player and records, but Luc's authoritarian father denied him his inheritance and his son never forgave him. Luc's artistic path was frustrated from the beginning. He was not given the chance either to study music or play an instrument, yet he never abandoned his dream. He established the classical record label *Phaedra* with an output of hundreds of albums of rarely heard and not previously recorded music, leaving a treasure trove behind, the progeny of his passion.

My grandparents, Lodewijk and Maria, were both orphans. Lodewijk's dad was Engelbert, the troubled composer who died young, the subject of my granduncle's book. Maria's mother was known as a batelière, a ferry woman. Her name was Veneranda Wauters—another widow with a big heart who raised six children on her own, while managing a tavern for the boatmen bringing freight to Mechelen. Long before I was born my grandparents had established a grocery store on the Ijzerenleen, wistfully fancied as the Champs Elysees of Mechelen with its eclectic 'traditionally inspired' patrician facades, rebuilt following the destruction caused by World War One, after a competition was held among the architects of the town. Lodewijk and Maria named their shop 'De Boterbloem'

(The Buttercup). In the old days cargo vessels delivered goods that would be hauled on a hoist into an adjoining double-storey warehouse on the banks of the Dijle River. It was a forbidden area for us kids, though my cousins and I rode the hoist up and down when grandpa wasn't around. Passing the shop every day on my way to school, grandmother spoiled my brother and me, and whoever was with us, with biscuits, 'borstbollen' for our imaginary sore throats, chunks of liquorice which she chopped off a large block, and 'neuzekes'—the cone-shaped raspberry flavoured purple delights resembling a little nose (neuzeke). My grandfather reprimanded her, but she kept doing it until he looked the other way. He too had a sweet tooth. You had to keep an eye on him at birthday parties. While everyone prattled and chitchatted grandpa would quietly finish off a tray of tompouce, petits fours and chocolate éclairs. Grandma was the first person I saw on a deathbed, silently hushed in and out of the darkened room, left with a photographic imprint in black and white. After she died Lodewijk moved in with my parents and the family of his daughter, on a week on/week off basis, and I shared a bed with him. The Eau de Cologne he used was 4711. Whenever I smell it I think of him. Albert, the author, observed of his father, Engelbert, that later in his life big things became small, and small things appeared big. And so, it was with Grandpa who was seen by his grandchildren in his old age, as a somewhat comic figure. We giggled when he fell asleep at the dinner table and retold the story that when Lodewijk cycled to school one morning a lady emptied a bedpan through the first-floor window, soaking Grandpa in piss.

Yet, I was always in awe of him. He represented another era that children rarely heard talking about, and the stories painted a different picture than the one of the docile and hardworking shopkeeper. He outlived two world wars. Louis was the first one to drive a car in Mechelen and went on honeymoon to Istanbul—something that really impressed me. A miniature copper camel adorned the mantlepiece of our dining room for as long as I remember. Grandpa loved music—and loved cigars. And just like the Eau de Cologne, I think of him when I smell cigars. Once, for my grandmother's birthday, he presented her with a case of cigars under the pretext that she enjoyed the perfume when he smoked them. Grandpa, as many men did then, left the children under the wings of women. While my memories of him are superficial and elusive, my grandma Maria has always represented kindness incarnate. Like her mother Veneranda, and like my great-grandmother Theresia, my grandmother had a heart of gold.

I finished writing these reflections about bloodlines and family trees and switched on the TV to catch the late-night news, tumbling into the nepotistic circus on view at the 2020 US National Republican Convention, where half of the speakers are unelected and unqualified members of Donald Trump's family: his wife, sons and daughters, even the girlfriend of his son, spewing volumes of lies and fearmongering, interspersed with cries for freedom. My ancestors were tame compared to this lot, where sister and wife whisper slander and cousins write books revealing the truth behind Donald Trump, his criminal past of robbing employees and abusing women, his racist and abusive father posthumously analysed by the pundits of the world. Some family trees do indeed require some heavy pruning. How many kings and emperors of our glorious histories were assassinated by their sons who were slain in turn by their own offspring? How kind and gentle my father was in comparison. And with these sobering thoughts I went to bed.

8

THE PASSING OF FRIDAY 15 JANUARY, 2021

Shadows slump and sag. The pitiless sun has sapped the energy out of the day. The distant ocean hums and grumbles like a Soviet factory over the hill in a town asleep, but right here, outside my window, the breeze rules, dazzling the foliage, shaking up the leaves, newly polished to a glimmer by the afternoon's penetrating rays, whipping up a dance of light and shade, of fire and slumber. Somewhere in the neighbourhood a raised voice ruffles the languid brilliance. The forest echoes with receding bird call, like stones flitting over a lake's surface. The day already knows the battle is over, but won't admit it. Night is lurking behind the horizon. They eye each other across the fading sky, the young wolf and the old, each waiting for the crack in time when eternity is suspended, a passage through a no-man's land where the spirits of twilight hover and swoop like bats that some can see but few can catch.

9
MY LIFE IN A BOX

I DON'T REREAD MY DIARIES OR SEEK TO RETURN TO the good old days. Diaries are like toilet paper. I use them to digest my thoughts and relieve myself. I mentally discard them, though I haven't flushed them. The black cardboard box from Ikea remains at the back of the top shelf of my cupboard, heavier by the year. But this morning, I needed to check a date and brought it down. Randomly leafing through ringed notebooks filled with daily observations, activities and reflections, lists of songs or vows, pages decorated with memorabilia, drawings, poems and photographs, I was lured into a quicksand of memories and unwittingly a dam of emotions burst within me. My heart swelled and I was sobbing. Here was my life in a box. All my joys and my tears, the farce and the scars, the love and the loss fitted into a small Ikea box. How insignificant my tiny life is in this immense universe! How seriously we take ourselves. I am a sentimental guy. I cry at the movies. Looking at these photographs of another me, and of dear ones in times long gone, the shock of the passing of the years and the absence of those that have left overwhelmed me. I found the date, closed the books but a picture fell out. It showed my mother holding me as a baby in a time of war and destruction.

The Everly Brothers were the first live music act I saw and I couldn't believe that my mum surrendered to my begging and took me to the Ancienne Belgique Theater to see Don and Phil. My mother wasn't the musical one. My dad was. Still, here we were on the train to Brussels. I was fourteen, just my mum and I, a rare event in our family of four children. Phil was eighteen and Don just twenty. They were cool as. *Wake up little Susie* and *Bye Bye Love* had given me the jitters when I'd heard them on the Wurlitzer juke box in a milkshake bar in Hofstade. I didn't know whether there were cascading waterfalls in the mountains of Kentucky but that was what their voices sounded like to me. They transported me there. In my bedroom I learned to strum that fierce rhythm guitar of *Wake up little Susie*. I knew the songs by heart before I was taught English in high school. And so, my heart was thumping as my mother and I took our burgundy velvet seats. But during the 1950s the 'variety shows' were still the fashion. The Everlys only got to sing three of their hits among cabaret artists, a couple dancing tango and a magician of which I have little memory. It was over so quickly I had to question my mum endlessly on our return journey to convince myself that the magic event had actually happened.

As the train of my life rolled on and I grew a little wiser the legend that took centre stage on the throne of my memory was my mother, while the Everlys turned into her page boys. My mother, who knew me so well in spite of my absence from most of her life; who threw away my boots of Spanish leather because she deemed them 'not proper wear' for a judge's son; who pinned tiny flags on the world map to trace my wanderings; who always wrote and never gave up on me; who was the last person hanging at the bar at two am after our concert in the City Theatre of Mechelen; who dreamt of gardens and whose ghost sits beside me every time I sit in my garden in a continent she's never known. My frail mother, who kept herself alive until I returned to see her one last time; who my brother and I carried up the three steps into my sister's house; who didn't recognize me when I left the hospital on that last afternoon. My sweet mother, to whom I should having given more of my time and more of my love.

10
THE LETTER

THE HONEYED VOICE OF PANDIT AJOY CHAKRABORTY alights slower than a leaf growing, uncoils like a diamond python and wraps itself around my mind, tightening my awareness of the yoga asanas I do for my morning practice on a fleecy Persian carpet in front of the bedroom mirror. Parissa won the carpet at the Dolphin Awards as a prize for the Best Jazz Song of the Year 2012 and so it has landed, all the way from Shiraz, into our bedroom in Byron Bay. A magic carpet it must be. Many years ago, I crossed Iran in trucks and buses, from west to east, on my way to Afghanistan, but never visited Shiraz, nor Isfahan. We had planned to travel there this year to celebrate our anniversary, but the latest American Warmonger-in-Chief is trying to provoke a conflict with the ancient empire and oil producer, and my wife became apprehensive. Shiraz remains a dream.

Indian classical music has always been a passion and Ajoy Chakraborty has contributed much to my peace of mind and brought ecstasy to my soul, which is what makes life worth living. He calms me, then guides me from tranquillity into rapture. A topflight improvisor, surely a match for Charlie Parker's saxophone. Indeed, after a sizzling performance with the Jazz Masters at the Preservation Hall, the birthplace of jazz, he was declared an Honorary Citizen of New Orleans. Outside, the winter sun is mild, the bush turkeys have commenced their courtship ritual early this year, chasing each other around the garden, now and then jumping on the corrugated iron roof above me. Still, nothing can distract me as I sit and listen, transported by the deep voice of Ajoy back to India in the year 1971. Meditating on a busy railway platform in Bihar. Monsoon. A state in flood. A country on war footing.

These days the world is swarming with backpackers, but during the 1960s and 70s few were journeying to India, and many were seekers, travelling on a shoestring, guided by the grapevine of rumours from the pilgrims ahead. There were, as yet, no travel guides with lists of places to sleep and sites to see. The young artists and students of the times had graffitied the pretty 1950s wallpaper of smiling roses with anti-war slogans, bulldozed its bogus walls, build barricades, rocked manifestos of love and defiance and unlocked the doors of perception. Scientists dropped out. Philosophers dropped acid. House-wives abandoned their vacuum cleaners. Bras were burned. Free sex was on offer. In a good mood, God had given the girls the pill and the church did not like it. Priests dropped their black soutanes and got married. Questions were on everyone's lips. Gurus were found.

In December 1968 my first wife Beatrice and I had returned from two years of study and rough travel in Africa to a home town that appeared to have sprung from a fairy tale of the Brothers Grimm. Five centuries of grime and coal dust, seeped into the sandstone of the cathedral, the great council where my father presided as a judge, the city hall, the palace of Margaret of Austria, abbeys, beguinages and every shop and home in Mechelen was concealed with a mantle of snow. It was an enchanting return. The Miniature Theatre invited me to perform and we scouted for a place to live. But my parents disapproved. The theatre had, in our absence, hosted a play that had been highly controversial in our conservative town.

— 'I don't want you to perform in that theatre in my town', declared my father.

My mother agreed. The family name and reputation of the judge were at stake.

— 'Would you rather we move to another town?'

The answer was positive and Beatrice and I found ourselves a small apartment in Antwerp.

— 'This is the home of a labourer' my father announced, during the only visit we received, and he refused to eat the curries we had prepared.

And so, I drifted into the bohemian community of the great port city. We both took some temporary work while I studied, preparing myself for the entrance exams to join the diplomatic service. I wanted to get out, see more of the world. But one night, a few weeks before the exam, my house of cards collapsed when I came home to find my wife in bed with another man. Thinking back, I should have moved on then, but the pressure from Catholic families to stay together was too much. Divorce was unthinkable. No one in our families had ever divorced. Instead, we packed our rucksacks and hitched out of town to India to face the consequences down the track. I would not see my family again for almost twelve years.

We had been traversing India from north to south with the usual annoyances of rough Indian travel: bed bugs, dysentery, infections and hepatitis, each of us with a small backpack, mine full of Indian spiritual and philosophy books. I carried a guitar as always. Our six-month visas were running out. On our way to Nepal we passed through Bodh Gaya, where I did my first Buddhist meditation course in a monastery with the Burmese teacher S.N. Goenka. The ten days of silence and introspection were a revelation and Goenka gifted me with a technique of awareness that has helped me throughout my life. But there was a price to pay: a second bout of hepatitis. When I landed in Kathmandu I was in a sorry state and spent two months lying in a hotel room with a drip in my arm until being forced out of the country. I am eternally grateful to Yung Khan for having nurtured me through a precarious time.

It was in that emaciated state of anguish that I wrote a letter to confront my dad about his behaviour and received an angry and indignant response. During my travels I always kept up a correspondence with my parents, sharing my discoveries with them, even as they routinely ignored my interests and urged me to return home. In his reply he was scathing about my enthusiasm for eastern philosophies and insisted that parents knew best what was good for their offspring. My future lay in Belgium and with a decent job — end of story. We did not communicate with each other for a long while after that, though I wrote to my mother and knew that she would keep him up to date. For some years my only communication was with my youngest brother Luc and, even so, I had to send my letters to his wife's parental address since my parents did not like us to have any contact, fearing I would be a bad influence. My dad is no longer with us, and I regret the letter I wrote with a heart like a fist. I can understand where he was coming from and meant him no hurt. Such lessons come with age and experience, when the pumice of kindness has rubbed off the stain of resentment. Yet I also realise that the two of us in that little town of Mechelen was one too many.

11
VISITING MY HOME TOWN

I N MY SEARCH FOR ROOTS I HAVE BEEN DREAMING FOR a good while of an overdue visit to my friends and family in Mechelen, the town of my birth, but I have not yet succeeded.

Last night I was on my way again. I found myself near the Brusselpoort, the sole remaining of the 12 city gates built in the 13th century. I strolled along the Schuttersvest heading for the railway station when my path was blocked by a colossal building.

— 'Mechelen has changed since I was here,' I thought.

I stepped through a gate of sky-blue perspex and followed a wide corridor up to three lifts. I chose one that automatically led me upstairs. Two dapper receptionists pointed to a glass door and I ended up in a gargantuan Kafkaesque hall with young men and women rushing back and forth with folders and briefcases, or seated tapping and mousing, eyes affixed to screens.

— 'Excuse me!' I called out, 'how do I get to the Leopoldstraat?'

Everyone smiled politely. And continued working. I nodded and smiled in return, stepped through a smaller door, down some stairs and found myself in an idyllic garden, where two gardeners pruned roses.

— 'How do I get to the Leopoldstraat please?'
I received an encouraging smile while they kept on pruning. Moseying around the garden I found a fence that led into a cavernous kitchen, a hive of pots and kettles on stoves, pans on fires, cooks busy boiling, baking, frying. No one taking any notice of me, my nostrils inebriated with the riotous aromas and calling out 'Excuse me! How do get to', until I saw a ladder that took me in to an attic that turned into a silent library. Everyone sat reading, heads down, as I tiptoed through. A uniformed woman stood behind a desk, the mask of her face just visible above a sign that warned 'DO NOT DISTURB'. I decided to move right along and came upon a charming atrium that opened onto a four-door porch. I chose the third one, my lucky number, and landed in another office with a group of young men and women who were staring at their computers in deep samadhi.

— 'Excuse me. How do I get to the Leopoldstraat?'

I got a smile but nobody seemed to understand me. Well, you can imagine how it continued. I went up and down stairs, with lifts down and up, visited studios, auditoriums, laboratories, dormitories, a junk yard, crawled through a cupboard to stoop along an endless hallway with toilet cubicles on either side, until I came to a closed door. But, backtracking, I found a trap door into a warehouse, ended up in a small courtyard with sweating gymnasts, but at no time could anyone tell me how I could get to the Leopoldstraat.

My Aunt Lorette once said over a cup of coffee: 'Hasn't your coin dropped yet, Carl?' Well, Aunty, it did just now, when my dollar coin whispered in my ear: 'Carl, you are stranded in a labyrinth.' The offices, the corridors, the stairs, the doors, the gardens—everything started to seem very familiar. Had I already passed here?

The night progressed and I kept wandering around until a clerk stopped me and brought me to an office. 'DIRECTOR' announced the sign on the door. I knocked. An affable fellow with black hair, brilliantined into an Elvis cuff, and a pink silk shirt that was a size too small for him, grinned from his desk.

— 'Hello sir', I said, 'How do I get to the Leopoldstraat please?'
— 'Follow me!'

He led me up and down stairs, through corridors, patios, pagolas and paths overgrown with weeds, explaining that he was the only one that spoke English around here. Everyone else belonged to a Bhutanese Buddhist sect. Pleased that my mystery was finally cleared up, I gave my companion an amicable hug, as he pointed me to a small ladder into a sewer that led to a gate with a rusted sign: 'EXIT'.

It was with great relief that I looked up at the all-forgiving sky. I felt refreshed, renewed, as if the night had not yet begun. A landscape of hills lay before me until vanishing into the encroaching night. A twisting path led over granite rocks, through dense bushes under the menacing silhouettes of gnarled trees. I set out resolutely. And so the hours progressed as I marched, climbed and descended, fast-footed, stumbling and lurching until I reached the corner of the Leopoldstraat.

The Leopoldstraat was unrecognizable. I found myself in a sc-fi scenario a la Bladerunner. Metro trains floated above the cobblestones. Laser beams flashed advertisements. Lanterns in all colours flickered far above my head. A mass of people was shoving and pushing in all directions like a compass gone mad. I did not know where to look first. I had planned to start my arrival in the town of my birth with a surprise visit to the homestead where I grew up and where my brother now lives, but in order to reach the house I had to cross the Leopoldstraat first. This was no longer possible. With no other choice, I boarded a silver subway bullet that delivered me, to my delight, at the railway station of Mechelen. My heart was beating fast. An encounter with my friends and family would soon be a reality.

I ambled through the Leopoldstraat in good spirits, passed the residence where my grandparents once lived—a long time ago but still fresh in my mind—their beautiful garden now a Big Mac Take Away, adjoining a Space Bar from a Star Wars film. I looked for my aunt Madeleine's house. It had become a Zara shop. There was no trace of the building where I was born, when my parents' home, a block away, was acquisitioned by the German occupier. And the dwelling of my childhood friend, Frieda, had been usurped by a shopping mall with a metro station. I could not believe my eyes. How long had I been away? It was then that a woman came up to me and started kissing me with some ardour. It was not unpleasant, but I was surprised.

— 'Don't you remember me, Carl?'

Had I met her before? I wasn't sure, so I kept walking, determined, a man on a mission, until I stood in front of a large gate of sky-blue perspex. I stepped through it and followed a long corridor to three lifts. I chose one that swiftly brought me upstairs. Two young women at a desk with switchboards pointed to a glass door and I ended up in a huge Kafkaesque office with young men and women who were busy going back and forth. They were friendly and smiled when I asked:

— 'Excuse me. How do I get to Leopoldstraat?'

I could have sworn that these young people belonged to a Bhutanese Buddhist sect and realized that I had ended up in the labyrinth again. The thought woke me from my dream. So, forgive me, my dear friends and family, for leaving it so long to visit you, but it is not for want of trying.

FLIGHT OF THE CONDOR

1
IN SEARCH OF LOST MEMORIES

In my search of lost memories, I lost myself, wandering among the tombstones and unkempt gardens, weeds up to my knees, to find myself in an overgrown backyard of a small house on a steep cobblestoned street in a village in the Yunga mountains in northern Bolivia, sitting on a rickety chair at an unstable table below a mango tree whose roots had cracked the white adobe back wall of the house. Bees zoomed around the flowers of the passionfruit vines. Chickens scratched at the barren ground among the banana trees. I studied a foreign language I knew I would need soon, a necessary key to open the gate to somewhere else that would help me forget.

It was around noon. The sun was high and left no shadows. Vultures soared above slivers of clouds like wandering spirits and I wished I could see as far as them, beyond these mountains, beyond this sleepy afternoon, into my future. The past was a smouldering ruin. I set fire to it all myself. Across the vast ocean, I had built a log hut beside a shimmying, fast-flowing creek, ringed by forested ridges. It was my garden of Eden until Shiva, the unpredictable god of destruction, came causing chaos and confusion. The eucalypt forests I once called home craved fire to regenerate.

My time was up, my task fulfilled, my dreams erased. It was a year ago now and I had not met any other god or goddess since, and was not going to wait around. An Andean condor, the Sun King, ruler of the Upper World, hovered right above me, as if waiting. I looked up into fierce light until I was lifted, holding on to the ruff of soft white feathers at the base of the giant bird's neck, and was carried far to the east of here, across snow-capped peaks and glaciers, jagged cliffs and narrow river valleys that vanish beneath the swaying canopy of rainforests, soaring on the winds over mountain ranges, muddy rivers and waterfalls cascading silver in an ocean of green, the sweeping swamplands of the Pantanal, savanna country and cattle ranches, colonial towns and the quilombola villages of the descendants of slaves, the cerrado country of the Matto grosso, the land of the ancient tribes, the Xavantes, Karajas, Krenak, to Minas Gerais, land of the Mineiros.

2
SAUDADE

TO THOSE WHO LEAVE WELL-TRODDEN FOOTPATHS accidents are bound to happen, so when an opportunity offers itself and the cage is left open, the bird has to choose between the pleasant, the familiar and secure, or the unpredictable risk of the unknown. Now I have happened to find my cage door open before, but often when in flight, because the cage had caught fire. But this time was different. The pleasant familiar was a sleepy tropical village on the Bahian Atlantic coast of Brazil where my four-year-old son Tashi and I had enjoyed a quiet life among the fishermen. It was downtime after six months, travelling across the Pacific Ocean, pausing in Fiji, Tahiti and Easter island, through Chile, Peru and Bolivia, alternating bursts of casual work as a musician in bars, clubs and on the streets with slow gear parenting time among village people, shepherds and fishermen, the back bone of humanity, preoccupied with survival, toil and children.

The cage on fire I had left behind had been my first attempt since leaving home at planting new roots, cutting bloodwood and tallow trees to build a split level log cabin for my little family, terracing and planting orchards and gardens, making a home out of 500 acres of eucalypt-

covered ridges and rainforest gullies in the catchment area of the Ellenborough river, between the escarpments of the Bulga and Comboyne plateaus on the mid-north coast of New South Wales in eastern Australia. It was a tough life, but we were living a dream, chasing a utopian vision of the 1960s mind-expanding revolution. Back to the land. Living with the seasons, working with our hands, bathing in the river, cooking on an open fire under the cold southern stars or during a pause between deluges of tropical rain when the creeks flood the flats and rage like angry water devils. Nameless days, timeless days, immersed in the omnipresence of the woods, the wind in the creaking trees, the rushing of the rapids, the abundance of wildlife, nesting with a newborn, in harmony with nature. The rewards, the trials of learning and the endless discovery of the world around me and within me, eclipsed the hardship and labour, lack of electricity and isolation. I felt I had finally come home.

We were not totally alone. A handful of kindred 'hippy' pioneers were doing the same in adjoining valleys, on the Bulga plateau and by the Doyles river, all of us building cabins and having babies, planting fruit trees and crops, sharpening axes and chainsaws, struggling to start tractors, sweltering under the sun or cut off by the floods. *The Whole Earth Catalog* was our bible, the *Book of Tools* with its advice on carpentry, gardening, masonry and welding equipment, design, sources and resources to aid the do-it-yourself man. We were all learning how to survive—exchanging expertise, swapping tools, sharing trucks and joining forces in working bees to erect barns, build dams or roll out barbed wire fences to keep wallabies from our seedlings. I experienced the meaning and the generosity of Australian mateship firsthand. The more energy one spends the more there is to burn and the full moon parties were shaking the barn, the old folks getting down, smoking home grown and jumping to real live music while the kids slept on mattresses in the barn. I joined my friends Enver and Dirk, who frailed* the banjos, strumming my mandolin for the bluegrass tunes, and sang the popular country rock favourites of the day by bands with names like the Ozark Mountain Daredevils, the New Riders of the Purple Sage, the Flying Burrito Brothers and the Nitty Gritty Dirt Band.

Then my partner left. One day I was a pioneer farmer far from the madding crowd, the next day I became a single parent of a three-year-old boy. I leased the farm, bade goodbye to friends, gathered our toys and instruments and went east. I hold dear memories of that precious time and my heart was taking time to heal.

The risk of the unknown was an offer from my dear friend Fernando da Motta to come to Minas Gerais, a mountainous state of verdant valleys and arid ranges far from the Atlantic coast, the home of twenty million Mineiros, a land of waterfalls and geysers, hot springs and medicinal waters, mystics, poets and UFO sightings, steeped in Catholicism and legends, pillaged and plundered by the Portuguese kings, hungry for gold, diamonds and precious stones, on the blood and sweat of African slaves and the bones of

---

FOOTNOTE: technique of striking the strings of the five-string banjo with the back of the fingernail and plucking the 5th string with the thumb.

Indians. General Mines, ruled by the gun, corralled by the cross. 'But these days' Fernando told me, 'Minas Gerais is the centre of one of the most important contemporary movements of Brazilian music, with a treasure grove of musicians and composers: 'the *Clube da Esquina* or The Corner Club of Milton Nascimento', Lô Borges, Wagner Tiso, Toninho Horta, Fernando Brant, Beto Guedes, Flávio Venturini. Fernando had his finger on the cultural pulse of Minas. He knew everyone and was equipped with the charm of a renaissance diplomat, the eye of an architect or film director, the playful and musical soul of an artist. Women found him irresistible. He offered a good ear, a kind and helping hand and an emperor-sized bed, more popular than any Hollywood mogul's matrass. Fernando had a generous heart too. He offered us his bed and I wore his clothes. We shared a love for the ninth art of comics.

Fernando would become my brother. We would be bound by what the Japanese author Haruki Murakami calls 'artificial blood'.

With no particular place to go, besides a vague plan to travel eastward and eventually visit my parents, sister and brothers after a hiatus of eleven years, I seized the moment, and this time I did not leave a burning cage. The ancient Greeks had a name for it: kairos. The opportune time that calls for action. The fateful decision at the crossroads. And so, we swapped a tranquil beach paradise for a vibrant city of five million inhabitants, the capital city of Belo Horizonte, or Beaga after the Portuguese pronunciation of the letters B and H. Surprisingly, my musical career started within hours of our arrival. It was a case of being the right man in the right place. That weekend I played my first show, member of a six-piece band, at La Taberna, a Spanish casa de show, where I befriended many of the musicians who would become close collaborators for years to come. My boy and I were instantly welcomed among these reserved Mineiros who adored the arts and loved their families and, almost at once, we switched to speaking Portuguese, even between ourselves. Language is the door into another culture, its secrets and sensibilities, and a key to belong. Through language we truly transform into a different person.

We found another traditional house with whitewashed walls not unlike the one in the village in the Bolivian Yungas. It also lay on a steep hill, the curse of taxi drivers who were called upon to move our drummer, Serginho, with his kit after our band rehearsals. We kept chickens in the yard, had hamsters for pets, then quails, tropical fish, a dog, and tortoises that disappeared for months among the roots of the banana trees. Our menagerie included a scorpion, named Doctor Venom, kept in a small aquarium in my son's bedroom, and a large rabbit that lived for years next to the fridge and bit every small child that attempted to pat him. Perna Longa was a rabbit with attitude. I suspected him of being a hare. He was a free thinker and kept one of our roosters as a lover. The rooster had no feathers left on his backside, and was the cause of embarrassing explanations from many a parent when Perna Longa mounted the rooster at kids' parties.

Tashi settled into a Montessori school at the bottom of our street, where I picked him up at noon to have lunch at home, or more often, in one of the many eating haunts along the Avenida Prudente de Moreas. I joined mums with young children at the swimming pool and dads with their boys at capoeira classes. At bedtime we read the stories of a boy who accompanied the Bandeirantes, the adventurers and slave hunters who during the eighteenth century terrorised the unmapped regions. And just like when I was a child, he possessed the whole collection of Tintin books. I had read them in Flemish, we now read these Belgian comic strips in Portuguese. There were school holidays on faraway Atlantic beaches in Bahia and Espirito Santo, in idyllic villages high in the mountain ranges of Minas Gerais. We stayed at Mario's bee farm, went horse riding on the coffee plantation of my friend Miriam in Santo Antônio do Amparo, swam in the rock pools near Mauá and the Serra de Cipo. Fernando had provided the key to a new life. We had planted roots, received an infusion of Brazilian blood. We had boarded the trem mineiro. Though the official translation of the word 'trem' is 'train', in the peculiar slang of Minas 'trem' can also mean 'a thing', 'any thing'. We had been accepted and felt a part of 'the Minas thing'.

As I write these lines visions of Minas, its colonial towns, with cobble-stoned streets and baroque churches, the isolated hamlets, forgotten when the rush for gold dissipated, give me a case of saudade, that ambiguous feeling of longing for what was once loved and is now out of reach. Their names sound like music to me now. Conceição do Mato Dentro, Milho Verde, São Tomé das Letras, Mariana, Serro, São Vicente, Lavras Novas, Araçuai, São Lourenço, Tiradentes, São João del Rei, Ouro Preto. Saudade is what the Bahian writer, Jorge Amado, calls 'the eye of the heart'. *Alegria* is its Brazilian opposite: the euphoric joy of carnival celebrations. Alegria and saudade complement one another and, like in the yin-yang symbol, there is a drop of hope in the sadness of saudade. Lovers who are apart retain a chance of reuniting. This wistful longing forms an integral part of the psyche of a country of slaves and immigrants who had little likelihood of ever seeing their homeland again. Saudade had travelled across the Atlantic Ocean with the Portuguese colonisers. Portugal too had saudade embedded into its soul. It was a country of *marinheiros*, seafarers, who often never returned. Saudade is the melancholic gene of the Portuguese *fado* songs, the code and the key to the mournful *morna* melodies of the Cape Verde islands, another ex-Portuguese colony. It pulls your heartstrings. And it has never stopped pulling mine.

3

TREM MINEIRO (THE MINAS TRAIN)
cop. Carl Cleves

TREM MINEIRO

Tantas noites eu sonhei
Hoje eu embarquei
Vou pra Minas Gerais

Sou um homem caseiro mas a vida me levou
Longe dessa terra Brasileira que me acolheu
As cartas, as fitas, lembrança
A raça, a dor e a dança
Vou pra Minas Gerais

Bota a cara fora da janela
Deixa o vento passar pelo cabelo
Sopra as teias desse violeiro
Com o som dos trilhos só falta um pandeiro
Adeus Corcovado, tchau Rio de Janeiro
Na terra do Mineiro não sou estrangeiro

Dumdumbe, Dumdumbe,
Dum vem de Maceió
Paulinha, ela vem do Maranhão
Zé de Salvador
Esqueci de onde eu vim
Sei onde vou
I don't know where I come from
But I'm going home

Tantas noites eu sonhei
Hoje eu embarquei
Vou pra Minas Gerais

THE MINAS TRAIN

Many nights I dreamt
Today I embark
I'm going to Minas Gerais

I am a homely man but life took me
Far from this Brazilian land that welcomed me
The letters, the tapes, memories
Race, pain and dance
I'm going to Minas Gerais

Put your head out of the window
Let the wind pass through your hair
Blow the cobwebs from this guitar player
With the sound of the railway tracks
Only a tambourine is missing
Goodbye Corcovado, farewell Rio de Janeiro
I am no stranger in the land of the Mineiro

Dum comes from Maceio
Paulinha, she comes from Maranhao
Ze from Salvador
I forgot where I came from
But I do know where I'm going
I don't know where I come from
But I'm going home

Many nights I dreamt
Today I embark
I'm going to Minas Gerais

Saudade virou um jeito de ser
Amar na ausência
O povo que luta tem o dom da alegria
Tem força e quando canta faz magia

Vou pra Pirapora ver o rio São Francisco
Ouro Preto, vou fazer papel de turista
Na capital vou trabalhar
Tocando violão num teatro ou num bar
Com a rapaziada encontro cada dia
Comendo feijoada, farinha, cachacinha

Com Beto, Mauricio, vou jogar futebol
Claudinha é pra cachoeira
Capoeira é com João
Não preciso me apressar
Aqui eu vou parar
Isso é meu lugar
Aqui eu vou ficar
Minas é meu lugar!

Longing became a way of being
To love in absence
The people that struggle, have the gift of joy,
Have strength and create magic when they sing

I will go to Pirapora to see the San Francisco river
In Ouro Preto I will act the tourist
In the capital city I shall work
Playing my guitar in a theatre or a bar
Everyday I'll meet my mates
Eating feijoada, farinha, cachacinha*

With Beto, Mauricio I'll play soccer
I'll take Claudinha to a waterfall
I'll practice capoeira* with Joao
I don't need to hurry
Here I will stop
This is my kind of place
This is where I'll stay
Minas is my place!

- feijoada: dish of pork leftovers and beans
- farinha: rough corn flour
- cachacinha: sugarcane spirits
- capoeira: Brazilian martial arts from the black slave tradition

A BRAZILIAN TWIST

WITHIN A YEAR OF OUR ARRIVAL IN BRAZIL, I had run into problems with the federal police. After the first six months, when the second extension of my tourist visa had run out, Tashi and I had been forced to travel the long journey to Paraguay to obtain a new entry visa. After this second visa expired, a renewal was denied. My Australian 'trespassing' conviction resulting from an environmental protest at Middlehead beach near Kempsey, had worked against me. Though all other protesters in the case were absolved, I had been convicted in absence and now carried a criminal record. Trying to convince a thuggish looking police officer that 'trespassing' is really a harmless pastime had been unsuccessful. He did not understand the word 'trespassing' on my document. As far as he knew I might have raped a child or blown up a nuclear facility. I did not want to get off the trem mineiro. I wanted to stay. Tashi and I had made many friends in Belo Horizonte during this first year, and all were sympathetic to our plight. Panic is not a proper Mineiro response. Slow wheels were in motion.

And so, I learned of the wonderful Brazilian technique for solving difficult problems called: 'vamos dar um jeito' (let's give it a twist). Actually, I had become acquainted with the technique soon after arriving and, at first, it had freaked me. The 'giving it a twist' was often a last-minute option to salvage a sinking ship, a desperate race against time that brought on a rush of adrenalin, and my disciplined nature, drilled in to me by foot soldiers of the Church of Rome, had been challenged. During a late sound check in Montes Claros, in the state's north, we discovered that the impressive speaker boxes contained no speakers. The 'twist' then consisted of a small army of enthusiasts scouting the town on a Saturday night for a replacement—with a full house waiting for the show to start. Some poor punter was persuaded to sacrifice his home stereo that our 5-piece dance band burned out within ten minutes. 'Dar um jeito' is a loaded expression. A backdoor entry. Wink. Wink. Nudge. Nudge. The 'visa' twist, however, involved a far more sophisticated campaign. It went like this.

My brother-in-arms, Fernando da Motta, was acquainted with a man whose sister was married to a man who worked in the office of the audiovisual department at the Federal University of Minas Gerais. That man was persuaded to arrange a small concert at his home—starring me—to which the Head of the Music Department, professor Bernardo Pinto, would be invited. The house concert went smoothly. Wines were drunk, connections made, and as a result professor Pinto promised to request a meeting with the Chancellor to state my case. I held my breath and waited. Our days in the country were running out.

After graduating in Law at the University of Leuven in a previous lifetime in Belgium, I had travelled to South Africa on a scholarship and acquired a degree in African ethnomusicology. It was my academic record that finally swayed the Chancellor. But more 'twisting' needed to be applied. The Chancellor now had to convince the federal police that it was essential that someone of my standing, though a convicted trespasser, would be given a residence permit to work for the university. To do that a fresh rather complicated chain of 'twists' was required to link the chancellor with some bigwig within the federal police and then the bureaucrats in the department of foreign affairs. Meanwhile we had to leave the country in a hurry and wait in Paraguay until the necessary papers came through.

For a second time in a year Tashi and I crossed the 'International Friendship Bridge' that separated the two countries and found ourselves in a small hotel in Puerto Stroessner, the supply centre for the contraband that smugglers transport into Brazil and Argentina across the appropriately named bridge.

Puerto Stroessner lies in the triangle where Argentina, Brazil and Paraguay meet at the most famous waterfall in South America: the Foz do Iguaçu. The border town was named after El Presidente Alfredo Stroessner, the general who had grabbed power in a coup and clenched Paraguay in an iron vise. Stroessner protected ex-nazis, who had fled to South America, and had given shelter to the Angel of Death, Josef Mengele, the head doctor at the Auschwitz-Birkenau concentration camp. This sadist had experimented on Jewish and Gipsy prisoners, sterilizing women, amputating limbs and collecting organs, submerging victims in ice-cold water to study their reactions while they died. Those who survived the experiments were executed. Mengele had been all over the news in Brazil after it was discovered that he had died in the state of Sao Paolo. It was a horror story that had shaken the country. The vibe of Puerto Stroessner, however, was as frightful as wandering around a huge shopping mall. For two weeks, my son and I shopped till we dropped, hung out in the coolness of the pension, waiting for a sign, walked over to the Brazilian consulate each morning and waited in the queue to hear: 'Não. Nada.' When the documents finally did arrive, a new complication arose.

On exiting Brazil, the Paraguayan border guards had insisted on a generous financial contribution. Since my passport carried the proper visa, I declined. They consequently refused us entry. After several hours, stranded in the mid-afternoon heat with a young child on the Friendship Bridge between both countries, I used the opportunity of a changing of the guards to sneak unnoticed across the border. We had already been illegally in Paraguay for two weeks. Getting in had been the easy part, but how to get out and reenter Brazil? The same Paraguayan officials now demanded an even heftier sum of money. I tried my previous trick and used the chaotic lunch-hour-traffic-jam around the border posts to stroll quietly across the bridge, carrying my backpack and guitar and Tashi his little pack. But when I showed the Brazilian military my passport it was their turn to refuse us entry. An exit stamp from Paraguay was missing. We were in the absurd situation of being trapped on that bridge once again.

There's nothing much to do on the half a kilometer-long International Friendship Bridge but walk up and down with nothing to eat or drink, keeping a low profile, well away from the guards on either side. It was a long hot afternoon. The only shade was in the cabins of the military guards and inspection areas. I entertained Tashi with an involved monster-and-dragon tale, with heroes escaping on flying horses, trees that whispered under a full moon, but time passed slowly. Tired and drowsy I slumped on the concrete, my son asleep on my lap, and recalled the fairy tale that was the life of Digno Garcia.

When Digno Garcia turned seventeen his uncle accompanied him to the port of Asunción on the Paraguay River to purchase the finest wood to build a harp. In the village of Morascué where Digno was born, his father had forbidden him to play the harp. Digno had patiently waited for better gods and mastered the guitar instead, while dreaming of harps. Now he began composing in his own innovative style. His fame grew rapidly and the young man toured throughout Latin America.

In 1953 when Digno reached the age of thirty-four the government of Paraguay selected the three finest musicians in the land to become cultural ambassadors and gave them each 3,200 dollars by decree to sail forth and promote Paraguayan music in Europe. The following year Digno, Luis Alberto de Parana and the king of the Guarani-song, Agustin Barboza, disembarked in Genoa. Completely unknown in Europe they travelled to Belgium, calling themselves Trio Los Paraguayos. During their first week-long engagement in the casino of the Flemish seaside town of Knokke, opening for French chansonnier Gilbert Becaud, the trio created a sensation and were instantly signed by the Dutch record label Philips. Their 45 RPM disc *Malaguena* reached number one in the Belgian charts in 1956. I was twelve years old when I heard it on the radio. I danced around the living room of my parents' house, imitating Luis Alberto de Parana's crooning falsetto in pidgin Spanish while strumming my air guitar to the precise rhythm.

'Yo no te ofrezco riquezas. Te ofrezco mi corazón a cambio de mi pobreza.'
'I don't offer you riches. I offer you my heart in exchange for my poverty,'

I admired the record cover in my uncle Fernand's music

shop as if it was the relic of a saint. Three smart men, striped blankets swung across the right shoulder, shiny black boots beneath a grey pantaloon held with a striped colourful sash, two classical guitars pressed against brocaded white shirts, Digno sitting down with his harp. Los Paraguayos performed for Onassis on his private yacht in the Mediterranean and dined on lobsters and oysters, unheard of in land-locked Paraguay. The trio toured Europe's most exclusive casinos, shared the stage with The Beatles and the Rolling Stones and appeared in the society papers with Salvator Dali and Imelda Marcos. Digno Garcia fell in love with a Flemish girl. He settled down in Geraardsbergen, less than fifty kilometers from where my parents lived. Digno had found a new home in the country of my birth while I was growing roots in the continent of his ancestry. When I heard *Malaguena* a dream was unlocked and I knew the wait would be worth it.

As night fell we managed to creep back into Puerto Stroessner under the cover of darkness and screened behind a line of waiting trucks, and retreated to our hotel to everyone's great surprise. For two weeks Tashi and I had spent hours in the dining room colouring books and making drawings. He had befriended the children of the owner. I had established a shady corner in the courtyard to work on songs and to study Portuguese. We had become a popular fixture and everyone had bid us farewell that morning with typical Latin affection. Now we were back. They were astonished by our exploits and cautioned us not to provoke the military. Over the following days I hid myself near the border post, spying on the changing of the guards, which I approached in turn to bargain. Eventually I received a good offer from a new face, put the cash in my passport, received the valuable stamp, collected Tashi and our belongings from the pension and, hand in hand, we crossed the Friendship Bridge for a final time, our packs full of contraband. The Brazilian Twist worked just as well in Paraguay.

On returning to Belo Horizonte I joined the staff of the Federal University of Minas Gerais in a research project of folkloric music. A team of graduate students had been dispatched to film and record the musical and ritualistic slave traditions, called *Congadas*, in villages and small towns in the interior of the state. Another musicologist and I were to catalogue the footage and compile excerpts on tape and video for educational use. The origin of the *Congadas* lies in the Congo, but, as with everything else in Brazil, these African rituals have been mixed with elements of Catholicism and local ingredients. Thanks to a 'Brazilian Twist' I passed many interesting hours in an air-conditioned office, peering at images of the crowning of the Congo kings and queens, the processions of Nossa Senhora do Rosário and São Benedito, the devotion of Santa Efigênia, the simulated fights against the Moorish invaders, the banners and masts, the dances and costumes, the declamatory chants and instruments: the zabumba, cuíca, caixa, pandeiro and reco-reco.

Murillo Fonseca, Carl Cleves, Julio Venturini, Renato Venturini, Augusto Renn

Marcus Gauguin, Carl Cleves, Mario Castelo, Jairo Lara, Ivan Corrêa

5
CINCO CINCO CINCO

A MAJOR BREAKTHROUGH IN MY MUSIC CAREER WAS a regular Sunday afternoon gig in a steak joint, called the Cinco Cinco Cinco, the 555. The band and I had started inside the corner of the steak house and, as the crowds grew, a stage was erected in the parking lot. But the punters kept coming and the parking lot swallowed the adjoining block of land. During the three years we kept a residency there, the owners built a roof over the whole car park, thus creating a huge venue for us. Their business had taken off and Sunday was their big day. Fifteen hundred punters, many of them students who came to study at the universities from towns in the interior of the state, spilled out into the Avenida Prudente de Moraes. Extra police were on standby. An army of waiters was employed.

The result of these shows was a spike in my popularity and a stream of invitations to perform in towns all over the state. Whereas before we had mainly worked in the capital, we now started travelling to distant places in Minas: to the old capital of Ouro Preto high in the Espinhaço mountains; to the western towns of Para de Minas, Dores do Indaia and Divinopolis; beyond the Canastra mountain range to the cattle-raising towns of Uberlândia and Uberaba near the border with Goias; east to Ipatinga, Governador Valadares and Teófilo Otoni; far north to the old diamond mining town of Diamantina and Montes Claros, known for its carne de sol (dried meat) and fine cachaça; south to the handsome colonial town of São João del-Rei. Now most weekends the band took to the highways and country roads to spread the word. It was all a little unreal to me, but I was enjoying rolling with the tide.

A feature of these Sunday bashes at the 555 was the gangs of street kids, called 'pivete' in Brazil, hanging off the front of the stage. Since there was no entry charge this free entertainment was not to be missed—and in the reigning chaos, difficult to control. Dudu and I always had to keep a close watch on our foot pedals, but the pivetes adored the band and I got to know a few of them. One Sunday afternoon those same kids used the moment to rob my house while I was performing at the Cinco Cinco Cinco. I tracked them down in the streets around Cidade Jardim and, sitting on the pavement, questioned them as why they would rob me while they came to enjoy my show each Sunday.

— "You are famous and rich. You know us. You are our friend, and we have nothing".

What riposte could you give to such an argument? After decades of military rule, the divisions between rich and poor were extreme and in 1985—the year we rode high in the Cinco Cinco Cinco—over half a million street children were institutionalized in Brazil. They swarmed all over the city. Some earned a few coins minding parked cars, doing menial jobs or selling cheap goods on the street. Most lived rough and were forced to steal from shops and markets to survive. Several pupils from the Montessori school that Tashi attended were robbed of their shoes or schoolbags after classes at knifepoint. I got myself in trouble one day when I intervened with a policeman who was roughing up a child, and found it wise to disappear from the Avenida for a few days. Many pivetes joined up in turmas, closely knit groups, as protection against the police. Some after-hours policemen were employed by shopkeepers to clean up the streets and between 1988 and 1990 4611 street children were murdered by police death squads. A policeman could earn $50 per child killed.

One night after the show, my band mates and I were sitting on the terrace of the Cinco Cinco Cinco, chilling out with a beer. Pivetes were hawking cigarettes and chewing gum at the traffic lights to the drivers streaming along the avenida when there was a screeching of tyres and a bang. A child lay bleeding on the asphalt. A woman holding an infant screamed and rushed over from the pavement as a car sped off. The child died before an ambulance arrived. It was a shocking end to what had been an upbeat day. It left its mark on me and I wrote two songs about the tragic incident. They can be heard on my album *All alone*.

6

FESTA JUNINA

— 'Que mistério é esse, que você tem
  Você leva saudade, deixa saudade também'

OSWALDO LIFTED HIS HANDCRAFTED VIOLIN UP TO my microphone, heaved his fat belly forward, his bow flying among his swirling coal black hair, and gave me that broad grin of an Indian, his strong white teeth glistening in the stage lights, his black moustache holding up his broad nose. Bowing while chanting the lyrics of this silly backwoods song in harmony, he towered over me, his ecstatic face pearled with sweat, smiling eyes squinting like a battle-tested samurai. I raised my black Gibson guitar in response, our eyes locked, and, in a farcical aping of that iconic rock cliché of the glitter twins, Mick and Keith, our mouths closed in on the mike and burst out together:
— 'Que mistério é esse, que você tem
  Você leva saudade, deixa saudade também'
The crowd roared with pleasure. Dudu watched us, leaning against his Mesaboogie guitar amplifier, cigarette dangling from his lips, while plucking the harmony lines to Oswaldo's fiddle. Dudu, stocky like a bull calf, never moved much, but

what his body couldn't do, his fast fingers made up for. I always teased him:
— 'Dudu, when it is your turn to solo, you are the star, man. Jump to the front of the stage. Drop to your knees. Hog the limelight!'

But Dudu never did. Once we sprayed his arms with glitter, so that the stage lights would make him shimmer.

'Um, dois, tres' screamed Serginho and hit the snare, ushering in the next song, *African Lion*, the tale of a hunting incident I had witnessed in Uganda that became the title track of my first Brazilian album. Flavio, tall as a maypole, skinny as rake, stepped up to the microphone beside me and blew the opening line on his alto saxophone. Mestre Caica, a mestizo ace percussionist from the Candomblé spiritual tradition, hit the single string of his berimbau, an instrument shaped like a bow, and pressed the gourd resonator to his bare stomach while Degas, our genius bass player sang with me:
— 'I don't know what it is that makes the world go round, there's talk of love and share-it-all,
 but I can hear the jungle-sound
 when the strongest tears the weaker down'.

I knew that very few in this audience here would understand the meaning of my English-language songs, but they could jump and dance to the music. And right now, the Praça da Liberdade was rocking.

Several thousand punters thronged around the raised pavilion where the band performed. It was on the grand tree-lined Praça de Liberdade, the true heart of the city of Belo Horizonte, capital of the Brazilian state of Minas

Gerais, that a market of artisans, the so-called *feira hippy*, was held each Saturday among the fountains and the flowerbeds, modelled on the famous gardens in Versailles. Against the backdrop of the Governor's Palace, the public library built by Oscar Niemeyer, the art deco buildings from the 1940s and modern and post-modern edifices from the 60s and 80s, each Saturday afternoon a known band was featured to close the market. We did this regularly. It was an honour and I was proud of my band. It featured some of the finest musicians in the city.

'A ultima!' yelled Serginho and we slipped into *Ragtime for the soul*, an exuberant country song that had been getting good airplay across the state. In front of me several couples were dancing forró. Behind them stalls were being dismantled and the sinking sun stretched the shadows. The show was over.

The instant we stopped Serginho started packing up his drum kit. The crowd still called for more, but it was 6 pm and we had to get out of the city in a hurry. A Volkswagen kombi van was already waiting behind the bandstand. Getúlio, the driver, helped Degas load his bass rig into the van. Dudu was chatting up two gatinhas, the spunky pussycats that seemed to be everywhere, while I sat on the stairs of the bandstand signing copies of my record. Caica waved me goodbye, carrying his pandeiro, shakers and berimbau. He would not be coming with us. Oswaldo had installed himself already in the front passenger seat, sitting upright, like an Indian chief, his rabeca (precursor of the violin, popular in rural communities of Brazil) at his chest like a sceptre. While Serginho and Getúlio were running back and forth with instruments, cases and boxes, Flavio and I bought grilled corns on the cob from a jovial woman whose granddaughter told us she loved the show. At dusk a sudden chill fell. Winter was coming to the highlands of Minas. We were deep into the month of June. I squeezed into the back of the van with my four band mates. At 7.15 Getúlio turned the van into the Avenida Bias Fortes to join the Saturday evening traffic. We had almost 200 kilometers to drive to the next gig: a *festa junina* somewhere northwest near Patos de Minas.

After passing the industrial town of Betim, home to the giant oil refineries of Petrobras and Fiat's largest car factory, darkness reigned over the savannah country, but for the occasional bright lights of small towns. We were heading west into the cerrado—dry country mostly suited for cattle raising. The headlights of the VW spooked trees with twisted trunks and the odd pair of eyes of a cow on the side of the road. There were no side windows for us to look out from. It was uncomfortable in the back of the van and the exertions of the show were taking a toll. Serginho was dozing. He was the newest member of the band after Mario left. Mario had been the drummer for African Lion. Years later I received the news that Mario had died from a heart attack, collapsing in the municipal park during an afternoon stroll. Thieves robbed my dying friend of his wallet and car keys. They then drove his car to raid his house. His poor wife and children not only lost a husband and father, but also came home in grief to a pillaged house.

Brazil is both generous and mean, a land of contradictions and extremes. I had instantly fallen in love with its warm-hearted people and had acquired many fabulous friends here. I adored its music, its poetry, the kaleidoscope of rich cultures spread across this vast country, half the continent of South America. Here I could spend a lifetime of discovery. But Brazil was also the place where trade union leaders were frequently assassinated by private militia, where shopkeepers in Sao Paolo bribed policemen who formed after-hours squads to execute the street kids that stole from their shops. Brazil was a country where a few owned much and many were left without land or work, struggling to survive in the slums of large cities. But in 1984 change was in the air. Democracy peered over the horizon.

Juno was the wife of Jupiter, the ruling goddess of the Romans. She was the symbol of love, fidelity and fertility, the protector of women. When Christianity spread from Rome across Europe the church tactically adopted the festive Juno tradition, passing her knack for marriage fidelity on to a man, Saint Anthony. The month of June was the month of harvesting crops and the Europeans celebrated the mid-summer event with parties, dancing around bonfires on hilltops, jumping through the flames, burning some of the crop to gain blessings for the next harvest. The Portuguese colonizers brought the tradition to Brazil. But here June falls in the beginning of winter. There is no harvest and the Festas Juninas extend throughout the month, commemorating Saint Anthony on June 13, Saint John on June 24, and Saint Peter on June 29. In the big melting pot of cultures that Brazil is, the Festas Juninas were welcomed by everyone—even the slaves and native Indians

—and many more traditions and costumes joined the party. The French contributed the official dance: the quadrilha, a kind of square dance in which the men dress up as country hicks with straw hats and braces and the women wear red-checkered dresses, don pigtails, paint gaps on their teeth and freckles on their nose and cheeks. Young men climb a greased pole to gain the prize of money placed on its top. At the Festa de São João, as it is often called, everyone dances to country music, the *musica sertaneja*, sung in harmony to the rhythm of the accordion and the viola caipira—a rural guitar with five pairs of steel strings—while couples dance around the mock wedding of a bride and groom. The greatest virtuoso of the viola caipira was Zé Côco do Riachão and he came from Minas. The Festa Junina is perhaps the most widely celebrated festival in Brazil outside of Carnival. The band and I had played many such Festas on bitter-cold June nights. In the city, four or more bars in a suburb pooled resources to organize a Festa Junina. The street was closed for traffic. Stalls sold *canjica*, a sweet corn porridge made with coconut milk, flavoured with roasted peanuts, spiced with cinnamon. Thick soups kept you warm from the cold. If that didn't do the trick, then try quentão: a hot brew of rough red wine or water mixed with cachaça (cane spirits), simmering in ginger and spices. The quentão fuelled your jump through the bonfire. A stage for the band was erected in the street and everyone danced. That was in the city. Tonight, we would entertain a small rural town somewhere out west.

— 'Take a swig, guys. It will keep you warm.'

Oswaldo turned his head and offered us sufferers at the

back, a small metal bottle with Grand Marnier. He and Getúlio had been discussing the qualities of a fine quentão, Getulio his eyes on the road ahead, Oswaldo stroking his moustache and tugging at his wispy beard. We passed the bottle around. Degas started on some anecdotes from his two years on the road with a professional dance band. These bands lived in comfortable trailers and travelled far and wide in the interior, playing six hours per night in every popular dance style: samba, bolero, tango, rock, reggae, foxtrot, frevo, lambada, axe, forró, cha cha cha, paso doble and baião. Degas snickered. He'd seen it all before. Our two and a half hour shows were a child's play to him. Suddenly, the van wobbled and began to swerve. Getúlio coasted the vehicle off the road. We came to a stop. Silence and darkness all around us.

Getúlio stepped out.

— 'Merda! Blown a front tyre!' he shouted. 'Everyone out.' He swung open the backdoor and we stumbled out. Stiff and cold, we rubbed ourselves, standing there like lost sheep on a mountain ledge. Getúlio was rummaging in the back of the kombi van by torchlight to save his car battery. We all watched as he lifted a heavy box of leads out of the vehicle. He took out Dudu's and my guitar and began shifting bags and amplifiers around inside.

— 'Oi rapazes, me ajuda, por favor!'

We all shuffled to the back of the van without much enthusiasm.

— 'Come out of the car and help, Oswaldo. You're the big guy', I said.

A bandleader needed to delegate responsibility. My friends

Renato Társia and Marco Antônio Araújo had taught me how to be the steersman, Brazilian style, when they saw how I initially had struggled to keep commitment and authority.
— 'You provide the work. You are the boss' said Marco.
— 'Be fair, but strict so that they are on time at rehearsals, well-dressed and primed for the shows—and not drunk. You must reward and punish to win respect. You will be everyone's mum and dad.'

Indeed, at first things had been chaotic. Someone was always late or absent, blaming woes with the car or the difficult girlfriend. A drummer snorted too much cocaine halfway through a show and the band struggled to keep pace with him for the rest of the night.

Now, in Brazil commitments are generally relaxed, but I needed to lift my game. I took my friends' advice to heart and gave the musicians a pep talk. Many bands struggled, but we had a lot of work. We had to become one of the best bands around to keep up this level. I vaguely hinted at replacements and stressed the financial rewards. And so, while I soaked up their *jeito mineiro*, they picked up some Flemish discipline. During the seven years that the band and I worked together I never lost a friend and, when the going got tough, it was to me they came to borrow money, pour out a bleeding heart or admit to a drinking problem. When not working we often surfed the nightlife together. We were buddies. When one is single, the hard-working all-male band offers a fraternity, only made restless by the aching for females.

— 'We don't have a jack', said Getúlio.

This was alarming news. We were in a hurry. Our next show was to commence at ten pm. Instruments and gear were strewn about in the tough grass on the side of the road. A dank fog oozed from the darkness. I could just make out the shape of the kombie. Flavio and Serginho looked sickly, the stragglers of a vampire party. In the distance the threadbare murmur of a truck grew into a hum; the hum became a roar. Getúlio ran on to the road to flag down the driver.

— 'Why was a truck transporting charcoal in the cerrado country of Minas Gerais on a Saturday night?' I said to myself.

The driver seemed equally suspicious of a gang of men with instruments in the middle of nowhere. He looked askance at us and went to get his jack. I strolled over for a friendly chat while Getúlio changed the wheel of the VW van—Dudu holding the torch.

— 'This jack is not the right size!' Getúlio moaned in despair.

He handed the tool back reluctantly. I thanked the sullen driver and soon all that charcoal was sucked into the porous night and we were alone again under the stark stars, shivering from the cold. Some of us huddled on the seats of the car. No one talked but for Getúlio, mumbling to himself while pacing around his van. I sat on my guitar case, looked at the sky and let my mind wander to another such bitter winter night at a bus station in the old gold mining and world heritage town of Diamantina, where I had played a solo concert in the magnificent Casa da Gloria during a 10 day music and theatre festival. I was following the scent of a lively girl from Salvador with cinnamon curls, saucy eyes and skin burnished like copper. It led me through the arid back country on buses and trucks, and eventually on the legendary trem do sertão all the way to Salvador. This old train, now no longer running, had brought so many desperately poor and landless people, escaping from misery and drought in the north, down to the industrial cities of the south, to find a place in some favela in Rio de Janeiro, São Paolo or Belo Horizonte. I lost myself in a tangle of memories of the warm reception of the black community, of shows around Pelourinho and of newspaper fame, of dance halls and swimming in the azure waters of the island of Itaparica, of thwarted love and the euphoric marching through the streets with the Filhos de Gandhy (the sons of Gandhi), the largest carnival bloc and afoxe group in the great city of São Salvador da Bahia de Todos os Santos. I was once again transported back, embosomed inside this colossal creature that moves and breathes, fueled by the sheer power and passion of thousands of men in blue and white robes, white turbans held with blue, bejewelled brooches, necklaces of rainbow coloured beads, dazzling in the hot Bahian sun, all striding proudly in parade , united as one, to the thunderous clanging of agogo bells, the rumble of drums and the Yoruba chants of Ijexá. My spirit returned to that state of bliss and ecstasy the arabs call 'Tarab', until the spell was broken when Getúlio yelled out repeatedly 'Merda! Merda! Merda!'

How long had I been dreaming? The night wore on and Getúlio had flagged down three more vehicles before he realised that Volkswagens needed Volkswagen jacks. Others wouldn't fit. Our only hope was to stop another Volkswagen, venturing out in this savannah country, way out west, on a Saturday night. There was little traffic on the road and the future looked grim. This time none of us could give our predicament a 'Brazilian twist'.

After two hours, São Cristóvão, the saint of motorists and travellers, who in Brazil is revered on the twenty-fifth of July with processions of trucks, took pity on us. He sent us a small VW beetle that stopped when Getúlio blocked its passage by standing and waving in the middle of the road. The frightened young couple, probably expecting a hold-up, were all too happy to lend us their jack. Stiff from the cold, we heaved instruments, amplifiers and ourselves into the kombi van and fifteen minutes later we were back on the road, praying to São Cristóvão that we would not suffer any more punctures. It was one in the morning when the van hobbled into the small town. All of us, except Getúlio, were asleep in the car when we were brusquely awoken by volleys of gunshots and an uproarious hullabaloo. The van came to a standstill in the middle of the main street, surrounded by a mob, banging on the doors and windows of our kombi van. The street was packed with people. It seemed like the whole town had been waiting for us. By now most were tanked and ready for anything. The passenger door was wrenched open. They dragged Oswaldo from the car. I'd never seen him with such a terrified expression as when he was swallowed up by this mob. Our sliding door slashed open and first Flavio, then Serginho, were pulled from the van. I was next. Half a dozen men lifted me up from the ground and carried me through the cheering crowd. Degas was heaved on someone's shoulders. His protestations were drowned out by peals of laughter. All around me guns were fired in the air and a worrisome thought crossed my mind: what goes up, must come down. I hoped these were not real bullets. Above my head a banner hung across the street:

'Festa Junina: Carl Cleeves e Banda.'

They never managed to spell my name right. My shirt came undone and I lost my cowboy hat as I was transported past a roaring bonfire and into a hall, also crammed with people. To a roar of applause, I was dumped on to the stage among my band mates—all of us in a state of shock. Oswaldo was still clutching his rabeca. Degas had lost a shoe. More vaqueiros—Brazilian cowboys—arrived with our guitars, cases with Serginho's snare drum, cymbals and kick drum and Degas' bass amplifier. I saw a woman with a polka dot dress and high-heeled leather boots, wearing my new hat, bought at the Mercado Central in Belo Horizonte for this special Festa Junina occasion. A huge man with a straw sombrero handed us all cups of quentão, which we drank to the cheers of approval from the mob. They were ready to party. Dudu slung his guitar over his shoulder. There would be no sound check, no speeches. It was that kind of night. Serginho grinned and counted:
— 'Um, dois, tres!' Oswaldo, Flavio and I looked at each other and burst out:

'Que mistério é esse, que você tem
Você leva saudade, deixa saudade também'

7
UPROOTED

LOVE IS A *PHANTOM*, MY SECOND BRAZILIAN ALBUM, was launched at the Teatro Cesciatti in the Palacio des Artes. I hung it in the smoldering gallery of past defeats and triumphs and hoped that now my heart could heal. But instead, my whole life in Brazil fell apart. The intensive workload had taken its toll. Crohn's disease, an abdominal inflammation suffered since my teenage years, caught up with me. While exercising in a swimming pool my intestine ruptured and I lost a third of my blood overnight. I was bedridden. Friends rushed to my side but could do little to halt my deterioration. Holding on to my breath, half conscious, I was taken on an apocalyptic journey into the heart of Goias in central Brazil to see the faith healer João de Deus*. It provided me with extra time, but my life was hanging by a thread.

I became emaciated and was forced to dispense with my band. I recorded one last song, *Penkele*, with my trusted mates and a thirty-piece choir, but kept fainting during the

---

FOOTNOTE: see: *Tarab. Travels with my guitar – Carl Cleves* – Transit Lounge publishing.

session. My time was up. All things must pass and once more I was destined to lose everything and be uprooted. All our precious belongings, Tashi's collection of Tintin books, his bicycle and toys, my record collection, instruments, amplifiers, the treasured souvenirs of our travels were disposed of in a fire sale. We gave away our pets, making sure that Perna Longa would not end up in someone's rabbit stew. Again Tashi and I had to bid our cherished friends and our happy home on the rua Mangabeira goodbye. It was the most painful farewell of the last eight years of travelling. Fate was playing tricks on me.

When I left Brazil my weight had dropped to forty-five kilos. I was dizzy with every exertion. A doctor in Rio gave me ten days to live. I had accepted the fact that my life might be over. It was now a race against the clock. My son was the first one to fly out of Brazil to Belgium, while I tied up the loose ends of the last seven years. The federal police, who claimed that my residence papers were not up to date, arrested me on my way out at the airport in Rio de Janeiro. It was a scam to get money out of me. I explained that I was very ill and without funds. They took my passport. The aeroplane was boarding for take-off. Was I destined to die in a Brazilian jail? The irony passed me by. I signed papers without reading before two federal police officers led me on to the plane in handcuffs. I was the last one to board and all the other passengers stared—and then diverted their gaze from my gaunt face. Perhaps I was a serial killer. It was an ignoble way to leave the country that had given me such a warm welcome. I was barely conscious during the flight. My family in Mechelen provided Tashi with a home while I was taken to hospital for blood transfusions and to have part of my intestines removed.

After a minimum of days, I left my hospital bed with its flowers on the windowsill, masking the gloomy, ashen winter sky outside. I had no insurance coverage here and all my savings, as well as a helpful contribution from my parents, were dwindling fast. Sunny Minas Gerais was a big hole in my heart. The stitches that ran from my groin to my stomach were a reminder of what I had lost, another marker added to the map of my body with its swollen ankle, broken and never healed, after a fall on the rocky banks of the Crocodile river in South Africa; the saw scars on the back of my right hand, self-inflicted when building the log hut for my little family on the banks of another river in a hidden valley of the eucalypt forests of eastern Australia; the razorblade cuts across my wrist when I attempted to end my life over a woman; imprints that stubbornly refused to fade after two decades of hard living. Physical recovery would take some time, time to reflect on the wounds of my heart that weep at night when I dream, time to study the twisted map of my destiny and the lessons awaiting me in the quest for meaning, belonging and for love. My kind-hearted brother Luc and his wife Monique nurtured us. A life had ended and the unknown not yet begun.

CHASING THE ANCESTORS' BONES

1

EASY LOVE

I SPENT THE MORNING EYEBALLING A SCREEN AND tapping the keys, a Maton guitar leaning against my desk. The house was quiet. The birds were not, calling out clear and sharp. But that is how I like it. I crumbed and fried sardines, steamed greens and beans with garden herbs and, after a quick lunch, drove to Lennox Head, a nearby hamlet on the Australian rim of the Pacific Ocean, to grease my suffering knee in the heated swimming pool.

— 'In preparation for next year's Tour de France', I told the ticket lady.

At this hour there was no one in the pool but me and I blissed out, a goldfish enjoying his private whale-size aquarium, doing forwards, backwards, sideways and knees-raised walking meditation, with the sun pouring through the windows, shimmering on the water. I managed a kilometre and came home, pleased with myself, ready for a little siesta. I had covered my eyes with the cat's eyes mask I bought in Melbourne and was dozing off, when my wife walks in.

— 'I am really happy with my haircut' she says. 'I think it looks quite good. And I am pleased with my new blouse too. This year my favourite colour is in fashion, so I might

as well splurge. It was on sale too!' She pauses and her other self counters 'Oh! I am so vain, don't you think?"
— 'It is ok to indulge oneself' I reply 'otherwise we all turn into Calvinists or Wahabists. All work and no play.'

She laughs and kisses me on the lips. According to some enlightened scriptures blindfolded kisses are the gifts of angels, and I can vouch for that. She sprays a refreshing perfumed lotion on my face and leaves singing. The thrill of her voice is the soundtrack to my life and my compass. However large the supermarket or department store, her singsong earworm in aisle twelve will lure me like a siren when I am lost. Sirens get a bad rap, but I have nothing to fear from this siren. She has wings, not a fishtail and I am a musician, not a sailor. I muse about how some Wahhabis declare that music is only meant for god, but surely no god could be so selfish as to deny humans one of life's greatest perks. An old gypsy saying comes to mind: 'Stay there where they sing; evil people will have nothing to do with songs'. I can relate to that too. Besides, I would never make a good Wahhabi since I venerate saints—like Howling Wolf, Jacques Brel and Caetano Veloso for instance—and the veneration of saints is not permitted either. With these ponderings I get out of bed and back into my office.

I sit down at the heavy wooden desk, bought for five dollars from a deceased estate at an auction in Sydney thirty years ago. How the removalists managed to get this colossus into my tiny office is a mystery. God knows how old it is. Every drawer produces little heaps of dust, but if there are any dust beetles I haven't seen them, so the desk stays. I would probably have to chainsaw the thing in half to get it out of here. The sweetness of my wife's teasing still lingers as her voice seeps through the wall of the adjoining office where she is coaching an aspiring singer through her vocal scales. Laying out a fresh sheet of paper it strikes me that the book of my life is happening right now, and thus I shall let it flow from the pen to the page in a stream of consciousness like Jack Kerouac and the Beats did.

'It's not so easy to write about nothing' says the cowpoke to Patti Smith in the first line that sets off her book 'M Train'. Looking at a blank page does not inspire, so I look around the familiar mess in my office. My triple guitar rack, computer desk, a mic stand and a guitar amp, leads and pedals, stacks of books, scribblings, lists and notes to myself, headphones, guitar plectrums and coins, my yellow fins and wet towel still on the floor, my treasured library and the figurines I have been collecting, every one with a story attached and with a life of its own. Collecting figurines is an ancestral predilection I share with my great-grandfather, Engelbert, the quiet man. My eyes land on the small plaster replica of the façade of a baroque colonial church, common in Brazil. Its prototype was introduced in the 17th century by the Jesuits to impress the masters' religion on the majority slave and Indian population and domesticate them. Mine is the size of a patio paver, a replica of the church of Santa Efigenia dos Pretos in Ouro Preto, the goldrush town and former capital of Minas Gerais. The church was built by slaves. Pretos means blacks in Portuguese. The plaster has been broken in several places and I have glued it back together each time, and though the frame is chipped and the towers haven't quite straightened,

it is still a pretty thing. Two towers, each with an open window showing a bell of hard copper-and-tin alloy, are separated by a decorative arch in the centre that forms the roof. The walls are lime-washed and the beams and frames painted corn yellow. An ornate portal for an entrance.

Santa Efigenia's church prompts the memory of a love affair at the tail end of my seven year stay in Brazil. Flavia was a beautiful woman and she knew it. An entire wall of her apartment was taken up by flattering photographs of herself, mostly in string bikinis. She was well experienced in bed, a party girl, charming and sensual like a Siamese cat that fixates you with a look, leaps on your lap, licks your hand, purrs while nuzzling your leg, then wanders off with an itch. A man magnet. I was just one card in her full deck, smitten with her, although I knew she did not treat me right. Somehow, I mustered the courage to tell her I didn't want to see her anymore. Though it seemed like a self-inflicted wound, I had felt proud of myself. For once I had imposed my reason on my lust and my own deceiving heart. What would have led to a sad defeat, felt like a victory. Flavia too was astounded. I don't think anyone had ever rejected her. Perhaps we both learned a lesson that day.

My teacher-priests at the Catholic high school of Saint Rombout never gave us instructions. There was no course in easy love. Yet, these skills would have come in handier than algebra or ancient Greek. Heartaches and battle scars, deserved or not, stalking the streets at night in a sorry state of neglect or wedded to the neurosis of work and cigarettes, were down payments towards earning the easy love, confronting egoism, fantasies and expectations, the stubbornness of my insecurities and the religious and cultural vocabulary of my upbringing. This took a good many years and more than a bucket of tears of self-pity.

Yet, somehow it all seems so simple now. But is it? It is true that some of us prefer our own company, but I have many wonderful and deserving friends looking for a deeper connection. What gets in the way? Where lies the path from romantic attraction to a deeper bond? What separates, and what joins us in our individual craving for fulfilment? We interact with each other on so many levels, our needs are varied and so are the roles we play. Seven billion men and women on the planet yield infinite combinations, each relationship unique, each individual with his and her own code. Is an enduring chemistry a realistic expectation? Or only a practical resignation? My great-grandmother Theresia, in a letter to her sister, wrote 'I suspect that almost all married couples, after some time, begin to live as strangers with each other, just like before' and concluded that considering the fleeting nature of love and differing essence of men and women, it would be best for men to remain alone. 'Men are more solitary beings than women', she wrote, 'for men there is so much that lies outside of love. For him love is a spur, an impetus. For women love is everything. For us it is a goal, for him a means.' Indeed, in the past men have been waylaid by power, ambition or thirst for glory whereas women, probably because they hold the key to the continuation of the human race, have had to focus on child rearing, especially in the BP days – Before the Pill. Yet I, as a man of many quests in pursuit of the unattainable, a trapper of unicorns, have always felt that life and love are connected like muscle and bone. Love is life's greatest lesson. Theresia outlived her husband by 46 years and remained alone. She was, like each of us, coloured by her own experience and trauma. But however deep the treasure map is buried, the setbacks and the wrong tracks, the handicaps and booby traps, the soul mate dream remains alive. Housewives write to dear Abby, businessmen buy books at airports, divorcees post their photos on-line.

Palm readers and fortune-tellers counsel on the pavement. Tarot gazers pull cards on fold-out tables at the markets. Philosophers and poets speak in tongues.

I don't really have a clue, but I wrote a corny Valentine's day song for my wife instead and it worked.

These are opening lines:
'You entered my room
The roses on the wall
Spilt their perfume
And burst into bloom'

And these are the final ones:
'Too much expectation only brings grief
But you've got to have a little self-belief
Always remember and never forget
It's the love the you give, not the love that you get'
(Good Loving)

2
A ROMANCE

TODAY WAS AN UNEVENTFUL DAY. Yes, I did yoga exercises for my troubled shoulder and knee. I played guitar, sang and blew my harp. Yes, I met my gang of philosophical friends over coffee in the morning on the terrace of the Bangalow hotel and we discussed everything but philosophy and, like most Mondays, found solutions to save the planet. I cooked a seafood laksa for lunch and cuddled my wife during a brief siesta afterwards. And yes, I buried the dead bush rat that has been lying in the garden since yesterday. Since no other animal has touched it, I conclude that it must have been poisoned.

It was indeed an uneventful day without high drama or tragedies, though with small pleasures. And in life we must be grateful for small pleasures. My final act was hanging the towels out to dry in the night, stars above like silver glitter in an upside-down sea of ink. Soon I will lie beside the loveliest woman I know, as I have been doing for years. And that is not a small pleasure but a wonderful stroke of luck. Hitting the jackpot, the fortune cookie in the lottery of Love. 'You wear rose-tinted glasses', she smiles. But I have worn dark sunglasses many times before and have concluded that it is better to focus on the possibilities that life offers rather than the fears or doubts. Starry-eyed? A falling star always comes as a surprise when you least expect it. And in the end, home is where the heart is, wherever place that may be. Let me tell you a bedtime story. Look through the rear-view mirror.

It was a long time ago. There was no 5G, no AI, not even mobile phones. No one knew what fake news or YouTube meant. A time before AD, the Age of Disinformation. He had taken a bus on Parramatta road, guitar case between his knees, and descended on William street. He planned to test a couple of new songs at 'Brackets and Jams', a popular musicians' night in Kings Cross, Sydney's own Soho of clubs, bars, strip joints, restaurants, drug deals, prostitutes, drunken brawls. Brackets of performances alternated with jam sessions. Original songs were encouraged and the place was always packed and lively with songwriters, students, poets, actors and punters. She was on the same bill, accompanying a Mexican singer. She wore a fluffy white peasant blouse, long black skirt, frayed at the edges, a pair of boots held in place with gaffer tape. Seemingly unrehearsed but beaming confidence, hips swaying, blond curls bobbing—she was a natural. She shook the maracas with such easy grace that his thoughts drifted to the bars of Rio de Janeiro where chorinhos and sambas reign. Her lyrebird voice instantly left a tattoo on his heart. She appeared to know everyone, so he waited, scribbled his telephone number on the back of his entrance ticket, walked up to the stage and mumbled:

— 'I like the way you play the maracas. If you are ever bored and feel like making music with someone, give me a ring.'

This had been his usual manner to reacquaint himself with the world of musicians in Australia's largest city after years of absence and it had resulted in several interesting encounters. Two months later, on a warm and breezy Sunday afternoon, the phone rang.

— 'Hi! This is Parissa. Do you remember me? You once told me that we should have a sing together when I get bored. Well, I've been drumming with the Brazilians at the Bondi beach pavilion, and I'm bored now.'
— 'Jump on a bus and come over. I am in Taylor street number 4, Annandale'.

He pulled out his songbooks and guitar and they sang until nightfall: South African trade union songs, gospel songs, jazz standards, blues, bossa nova, pop, country and rock. They chirped Rocking Robin and *The Boy in the Bubble* and were shocked to discover that both of them worshipped João Bosco and Hukwe Zawose. Who had ever heard of these people? He had never met anyone with whom he shared such an eclectic taste of music. The rumble of Sunday traffic on nearby Parramatta road receded as their voices drifted through the open window into the backyard gardens, across the canal and over the rooftops of the slumbering suburb. He hadn't had so much fun since leaving Brazil. He admired her breasts as she leaned over towards the mirror but knew nothing could come of it. She had told him that she lived with a boyfriend, who, coincidentally, was called Carl, just like him. He escorted her back to the bus stop. He felt he had made a friend. Romance wasn't in the cards. But fate had other ideas.

A month and a half later he got restless, needing to share some music to water his soul. He remembered that delightful Sunday afternoon with 'that maracas girl'. Perhaps they could do it all over again. He dialed her number. Carl, now her ex-boyfriend, answered his call. No, Parissa wasn't living here anymore. She had moved to the eastern suburbs. He gave him her number. She was thrilled to hear his voice and he was thrilled to hear hers. They talked for an hour like old friends catching up after a long absence. They discovered that they both intended to go on a holiday the following week. She wanted to head off to the country with Pascale, her house mate. He had the week off work. Why not go together?
— 'Let's take our guitars, make music in the forest or by the beach?'

He mentioned the cabin he had built in the forested ranges up north. It was still there, empty after so many years. She loved the idea.
— 'Why don't you come over for lunch tomorrow,' she said, 'you can meet my flatmate and we can discuss this further.'

That same night he phoned his trusty old mate John whom he had befriended on the island of Penang and who had been influential in getting him to Australia. John had built himself a shack in the woods a few kilometers downstream on a steep bank above the Ellenborough river.
— 'Oh mate! You can't take women there,' John said shocked. 'The place has been abandoned for too long. Windows are broken. There are possums and snakes in that house. You will terrify those girls. Go somewhere more civilised.'

Sitting in the shade of an overgrown bamboo grove in the backyard of her house in Waverley, he nibbled on her macrobiotic sushi rolls that fell apart as soon as you lifted them off your plate, while he tried to convince the girls to spend the holiday somewhere else.
— 'Why don't we rent a couple of rooms in a little hotel in Byron Bay', he suggested, 'we will be right on the beach and can sing to the waves'.
But she wouldn't hear of it. Pascale too had her heart set on his cabin in the woods. No snake, spider or possum would change their minds. They wrote out a list of supplies to take with them, dividing it up between the three. There would be no shops in reach during their time away. And no one possessed a car.

He met Parissa on the platform of the northern train at Central station at eight-thirty the next morning, both with guitars in hand and rucksacks on their backs.
— 'Where is Pascale?'
— 'She received a job offer last night and isn't coming. It's just us.'
Chugging along, high above the Hawkesbury River, they eyed one another. Besides harmonizing their voices months before, they knew nothing of each other and here they were going to a wild and isolated place to spend a week together. An astonishing circumstance. Unexpected. So they talked. She had left home at seventeen when her parents divorced and had signed up with an international brigade to go coffee picking in Nicaragua in aid of the Sandinista revolution but had joined a Peruvian folkloric band roaming around

Central America. He told her about his life in Brazil. She spoke good Spanish. He spoke Portuguese. She had sung in the *Voices from the Vacant Lot* choir before he had joined, but left because the rehearsals clashed with her work schedule in a macrobiotic restaurant. She now sang in a bossa nova trio. They exchanged astrological signs and worked out each other's numerological chart. The conversation flowed. Six hours passed like a flock of birds until they disembarked at Wingham railway station, marched out of town and started hitchhiking on the road to the Bulga plateau.

Hitching was slow. There was hardly any traffic and they got stranded halfway up the winding mountain road. It was a hot November afternoon and the hours were dragging on. He was an anxious man, sitting on the steps of Bobin Hall staring out over the silent road. What adventure had he pulled this girl into? Only he knew how far they still had to go. The place was practically inaccessible without a vehicle. The top of the plateau was miles away. From there it was another seven kilometers along the Colling Pass road where there would be even less, if any, traffic, and then down on a rough four-wheel drive track into an almost uninhabited valley. It was likely that they would have to sleep somewhere along the road or in the woods. How tough was this girl? He felt responsible for her. Protective. She was sitting between his legs on the step below and in a sudden gesture of concern he put his arm around her. Startled, she pulled away.

— 'Oh no! This guy is coming on to me!' she thought, 'What am I doing here with this total stranger? He could well be an axe murderer.'

Things were not going well. A ute stopped with two rough country bumpkins. They climbed in the back tray with backpacks and guitars and hooted up the mountain.

The sky was turning purple over the Bulga plateau as they walked over to an old railway carriage where Lincoln was living with his three boys. He hadn't seen his old friend in years. Lincoln handed them a beer and offered to drive them down into the valley in his dilapidated Landrover. The girl seemed at ease, but just as eager as him to reach their destination before dark. Night falls quickly on the Bulga plateau. The Rover dropped off the Colling Pass road on to the shadowy, gravely mountain track. Lincoln shifted into first gear. Wallabies leapt away from the bouncing beams of light. The birds had fallen silent. Only the motor growled its way down until it could go no further. It was the end of the track. They would have to descend the last ridge in the dark, torch in hand. It was a moonless night. Kangaroos thumped in the bush around them. An owl hooted. They stomped their

boots hard on the rough floorboards to frighten off unwanted visitors and shone a light in every corner of the hut. The floor was covered with pellets of possum shit, but there were no snakes. They lit some candles, found a broom and swept the house. He offered her the only bed. Then they kissed.

They remained hidden from view for a week, far from the madding crowds, singing, playing, meditating, swimming naked in the creek, exploring the woods, cooking on an open fire: oats, curries of lentils, chickpeas and rice, spaghetti with cans of tomato sauce. Making music, making magic and making love, in the same log hut where his heart was broken in another lifetime. He had come full circle.

3
MEETING AUNT SPIRIDOULA

September 10, Corfu, one of the Greek Ionian islands

Last night Parissa and I lugged our backpacks and guitars on cobblestoned alleys—too narrow for a car to pass—pausing to gasp for breath, past pallid streetlights into somber passages, drenched in sweat, heaving up the steep staircases of the old town of Kerkyra. Straining up the stairs to the first-floor apartment the door flew open and a stocky dark-haired woman threw her arms up in the air, yelling words I didn't comprehend, and grabbed Parissa in tight embrace. Thea Spiridoula is Parissa's seventy-eight-year-old Greek aunt. They had not seen in each other in twenty years and tears ran free. We have embarked on a year-long world tour of performances while seeking to reconnect with our heritage, the branches of our roots, and this was our first stop. Aunt Spiridoula pecked me on both cheeks. She beckoned us inside her small flat, muttering in Greek, while Parissa dug up fossils from her childhood when she had resisted her father's Greek lessons with a vengeance. We declined a late dinner at this hour. I felt awkward that our luggage and instruments had taken over her small living room; but in spite of protestations, she gave us her bedroom, stubbornly insisting on sleeping on the divan. Spent, we soon drifted into a slumber to the soundtrack of revving motorbikes, shrieking cats on heat, pestilent church bells, a battle of radios and alarm clocks, and an argument of drunks.

The air is fresh at 6.30am. Swallows draw scribbles on the pale sky. The alleys are still deserted but for street cats. Neighbours wake, stick their head out of the window.

— 'Kalimera!'

Around the breakfast table, Parissa, Aunty and I sit with our dictionaries in hand. Thea Spiridoula keeps squeezing my cheeks. She came to kiss me goodnight in bed last night. We will share this little flat for several weeks. I think we are going to get along just fine. Parissa is blissed out from the emotional reconnection with her aunt. Her eyes are shining like a ten-year-old. I am learning about the little rituals of the house: always burn a candle before breakfast for Tony, Spiridoula's deceased son, whose slippers I am wearing; how to navigate the ingenious workings of the hot water system; and the essential rule of never putting toilet paper in to the toilet!

Parissa went to get her hair done at Spiridoula's daughter's hairdressing salon, so I get in a couple of hours of practice time. Can't sing too loud with the neighbours almost in my room, but then this is Greece. Don't be shy. At 11 am Thea Spiridoula returns. I walk down the alleys to the communal tap to carry drinking water up to the house. Aunty has weak knees. She gestures and chatters till I grasp that she wants to introduce me to her neighbours. Like those penguins in the Disney film *Madagascar* I smile and

wave a lot, a skill that comes in handier in life than trigonometry, and rotate the eight Greek words I have learned. Spiridoula has bought me some chocolate cake after Parissa revealed my Achilles heel. A dozen neighbours watch with approval as I eat it.
— 'Like?' says a woman.
— 'Friend!' adds someone.

From the walls of the house Jesus, Saint Spyridon and other interesting saints and ancestors look on with benevolence. Outside two radios resume a vicious skirmish.

It is midday. Parissa is back and Thea Spiridoula has kissed me already eight times. It's ok with me. We are getting close. Last night I almost drank the glass of water with her false teeth in it.

— 'She says that you are gold' says Parissa, who holds the dictionary.
— 'Why?'
— 'Because you give love to your wife—something some of the men in her family are not good at. Her own husband was so jealous she could never wear anything pretty. And Vicky's husband is unaffectionate and only interested in his work. Marina's husband reads the newspaper while she is pregnant, looking after the children, cooking and doing all the work.'

After a lunch of stuffed capsicums and tomatoes, salad, goat cheese and bread we settle down to siesta. The roaring tide of bikes, ghetto blasters and arguments has ebbed. Even the dogs are slumbering as I sink in to a deep sleep, sodden in my own sweat.

The town livens up again in the early evening. I accompany Spiridoula to a store to carry back a gas cylinder for the kitchen. The gas trip becomes a minor epic as I am being introduced to countless women who live in the Campiello, the ancient maze of narrow lanes paved with large slabs of stone, connected with stone staircases, crammed with small curio and artisan boutiques, coffee shops and eateries. Everyone teases her, pointing at me.

— 'Spiridoula has a new boyfriend!' they all say.

Night. I try to follow Parissa and Spiridoula's dictionary tennis match for a spell but it has been a long day. I take off Tony's slippers and crawl into Thea Spiridoula's bed. Above the bedhead Christ, the Virgin and Saint Spyridon are watching me. The Saint is no laughing matter. He is rumoured to have saved the island from the siege of the Turkey's fleet. Unlike the rest of Greece, Corfu was never ruled by the Ottomans but was incorporated into the Venetian empire. The island's architecture is Venetian and its polyphonic choirs are more reminiscent of Italy than Greece. The saint is omni-present in Corfu. I feel like I am being stalked. I better behave. Anyway, Aunt Spiridoula will probably come and tuck me in with a kiss. Who wouldn't want such an aunty in their life? Oh! But first I must walk down the dark alleyways once more, to the communal tap and fill the drinking urn.

4
A BUSKERS' HONEYMOON

THE AIRPORT BUS DROPPED US OFF AT THE Plaza Catalunya. It was scorching hot. I heaved my pack on my back, grabbed my guitar and gig bag and started walking. Parissa had brought so much luggage that she could not lift it all by herself. A kind Catalan lady offered to help her and carried the darabuka and guitar. We stumbled along La Rambla—the famous 1.2-kilometer-long, tree-lined boulevard and pedestrian mall in the Barri Gòtic, the old section of the city of Barcelona—weaving between the throngs of tourists and buskers, the busy sidewalk cafes and market stalls, overwhelmed by the deafening noise of jackhammers and drills, traffic jams creeping along on either side of the Rambla. July in Barcelona is the hottest month, and the height of the tourist season. Sweat stung my eyes, but I kept marching. I asked for the Calle Ferran and turned into a narrow street. Parissa seemed on the point of collapse. We'd had a thirty-hour flight from Sydney, flown over Sarawak, Tashkent, ate croissants over Poland, changed planes in Frankfurt. We were almost at Lisa's flat. It was on the top floor of an ancient building. We started shouldering our luggage up the narrow staircase. It would take several trips.

Lisa is a Londoner who had been living in Barcelona for five years, teaching English to the Catalans. She came to dance to our band, the Hottentot Party, at a hall in the hinterland of Byron Bay and invited us to Barcelona. The attic apartment had been fitted out with modern amenities: a new kitchen and bathroom glimmered beneath the antique wooden beams that supported the ceilings. The tiled floor reminded me of Morocco. There were cats everywhere, meowing in competition with the clangour of builders, renovating a façade across the narrow alleyway, and the roaring traffic below. Lisa reminded us to look after her cats and left us the key to the flat. We fell asleep, jetlagged, naked and sweating.

I am lucky to share the love of roaming, first with my son and now with my wife. To lay bare my buried memories of Barcelona I had to dig deep beneath the archaeological layers of my life, reaching back to when I was nineteen years old, sleeping out in the parks and busking on La Rambla with a Gibraltar monkey for company, saving up my fare to travel to Ibiza. I spent a night in jail in this city for illegal busking, when General Franco still trampled the country in jackboots. At fifty-four I was returning to Barcelona, to come busking again. We had left our house in the Bay in the care of friends, who would turn our cabin by the sea into a marimba factory and rehearsal space to the dismay of our neighbours, and forged a plan: to travel around the world, meet Parissa's Greek relatives, introduce my sweetheart to my family in Belgium, and then continue to Brazil to see my old friends, 'para matar saudade' (to quench my longing). We intended to be away for ten months, but, since we had very little money, we had decided to come to Barcelona first and busk, trusting that our ability to establish a rapport with an audience in any country would help us survive. It is what I had done much of my life and both of us had done together since we met nine years before. Rombout, my old buddy from high school, and Dirk van Esbroeck, one of Flanders finest songwriters and tango afficionado, would organise performances for us in Belgium; other friends would do the same in Brazil. Bo and I had hatched a plan: I would ride into the town of my father on a white stallion, slash the threadbare, red velvet curtain between us with my six-stringed sword and sing my songs for all to hear. For so many years I had dreamt of healing the estrangement between my dad and I. My father was getting older. He had loved music and I hoped my song would be my sword. But first Parissa and I needed to busk, and save up to get there.

The next morning we climbed down nine flights of stairs with our guitars and strode the three hundred metres to the Rambla, squeezed ourselves between an act of break-dancers and an African guitarist, and started singing. It was a fiasco. No one could hear us—unless they stood close enough to kiss. Hordes of tourists strolled past, ignoring us. The noise of the traffic on both sides of the Rambla, and the racket of renovations that transformed the Barri Gòtic into a building site, drowned out every word we sang. Parissa and I starred in a silent movie, screened during a soccer match. The African guitarist beside us had an amplifier on a trolley, as most buskers did. We sang a few songs and gave up. Parissa was in tears. What were we to do? How would we finance our crazy adventures? The competition on the Rambla was just too great.

The Rambla was a lively place to be in those days, long before the pandemic struck us all. Dozens of motionless mime artists, slathered in make-up, stood like statues in the blazing sun, allowing a brief gesture to reward a passer-by who deemed them worthy of a coin. One elf managed to cling for hours, without flinching, from a branch of one of the trees that framed the promenade. A couple, with arms and faces painted gold, was clutched in tight embrace and, five meters further, a princess posed in a portrait frame; a red Indian, a scarlet Satan, a Pharaoh and a silver guitar god stood frozen in the midday heat, vying for a second's attention from the ambling crowds of families towing children on the verge of tantrums, amourous lovers, Catalan beauties on parade, elderly voyeurs and well-to-do tourists dining at the terraces. Saxophone and djembe players took on the drills and jackhammers. A Peruvian folkloric group—ponchos, panpipes and charangos—competed with the high-heeled ballerinas of a flamenco troupe. A Catalan brass band blared, oblivious to it all, while couples circle-danced the sardana, holding hands, stepping in time. Among the flower stalls, cafes and kiosks with chintzy souvenirs, pretty parrots, exotic chickens, baby tortoises and doomed goldfish enticed the amblers. Hawkers sold cigarettes and balloons, Moroccan jewelry and kaftans. Card readers sat at tiny tables holding the hands of sad middle-aged ladies wanting to know where love was hiding. On the pavement homeless beggars lounged with their families of dogs while tourists straggled by in a daze, handing out coins to the string quartet, the classical guitarist and the Chinese puppeteer who manipulated a frog that played Bach on a tiny piano. It was time for us to retreat.

The following day we went on a reconnaissance, to make a study of the territory and see what everyone else was doing. Wandering towards the harbour, where Christopher Columbus, high upon his lonely pillar and covered in pigeon shit, points towards the sea, we met Armando. Armando was a real gypsy with a waxed moustache above a gold-toothed smile, and he was acting the fantasy part of a gypsy. A guitar and his voice were all he needed. We followed him around, observing his technique: capture the attention of just two or three tables, sing a couple of songs, pass your hat with a smile and move on. Armando was raking in the money. Here are the rules: wait a couple of minutes until the previous busker has finished, win the approval of the waiters with a nod, target the audience with a quick shower of panache—because there are too many demands on their attention—cash in and move right along. Later that afternoon we tried it out and it worked a treat. We started out with an extensive repertoire but soon narrowed it down to just two brief songs in a blaze of fireworks and established a routine, hitting the avenue two or three times daily for an hour each time, before celebrating, with a wallet full of pesetas, in a fancy restaurant on the Plazza Reial, savouring a three-course meal, sitting at a table among the same tourists who had paid for our meal. Within a few days we had acquainted ourselves with the familiar acts: the intense santoor player, the electric guitarist who repeated a marvellous version of Sting's 'Every breath you take' at each terrace, the couples dancing tango with serious expressions, the muscular acrobats, the rows of portrait painters, spray-can artists, the students drawing the works of El Greco on the sidewalks with chalk, the flower sellers and stilt walkers. We had become part of the Rambla circus.

Sleepless nights. The narrow streets, with balconies that almost touch one another, echoed every sound upwards to our top floor attic.
— 'OLE OLE OLE!'
From the canyons below drunken English soccer fans—the World cup was on again—bellowed on their way back to their hotels at three am. Our furious neighbours retaliated, yelling from their balconies:
— 'SILENCIO!'
The thirteen cats in our apartment meowed at once, becoming hysterical when the church bells chimed over the Barri Gòtic. Cloisters, chapels, churches, a basilica and a cathedral surrounded us, and they all unleashed a barrage of chimes every quarter of the hour. Enormous medieval bells, just five meters from our bedroom window, boomed and clanged their way into our dreams. No earplugs could shield us from their thunderous peals. I woke in a panic fearing an impending aerial attack. The German Luftwaffe has returned. The placid old male cat was going berserk. I jumped out of bed to prevent it from a suicidal leap down the air vent. No one had remembered to synchronize the church bells and, between 6.55 am and 7.05 am, I counted eighty-eight strokes, before Moses parted the Red Sea of church hysteria to let pass the sonar assault of Vespas and

ghetto blasters, blaring romantic Spanish ballads with a disco beat. Sleepless nights in Barcelona.

Tossing and turning, Parissa gently snores beside me while in a Brazilian newspaper I read about the brutal murder of fourteen students. A photo shows their mutilated corpses as well as a gloating mug shot of the two killers: a mean-looking burly black dude who is the Chief of Police, and the Minister of the Interior, a short and skinny, pale Gestapo character with a nasty smirk on his face. I take a hike to the markets. Someone taps me on the shoulder and points. The Chief of Police is here in a dirty military uniform. Stained with what? Food rests? Blood? Everyone scatters and I find myself alone with him. He does not seem interested in small talk but focuses his glassy eyes on me. He suddenly becomes violent, pushing me and is about to beat me. I hurry off, fancying that with an AK47, I could easily eliminate him. But I don't possess an AK47; neither do I know how to use one. I struggle to get my car out of a bog, but manage to reach the next town. I sit on a terrace and order a coffee when I see a police officer study my car and write down my number plate. Merda! It is the Chief of Police. I break into a cold sweat. My days are numbered. My hours are numbered. How do I get out of Brazil? Surely they are on the lookout for me at the airport, the harbours are on alert. Can I make my escape to Paraguay or Argentina?

Clang. Bang. Boom.

I am saved from my predicament by the church bells. 3.15 am. Who should turn up but my cousin Luc Famaey. I have always been fond of him and am happy to see him. He tells me that he was born in 1928. My God, he is fifteen years older than me. He sure looks young for his age. I decide to do his numerological chart and rush across the road to my parents' house to collect my books. I never get there. It is 4 am and the church bells explode in stereo. Here I am in the Sudan once again, the guest of a Sultan. Or is that a Maharajah? A President perhaps? He has organised a symposium on literature. How thrilling! He doesn't look Sudanese. Maybe he is an Armenian. I have heard the rumour that he is a violent despot but he seems like a likeable family man to me. A group of students is assembled in an impressive Bedouin tent in the desert. We are holding our literary scrolls and I admire the timetables with a pretty Indian princess. We shuffle endlessly to find our seats until we notice that the venue has now shifted to a busy street adjoining a bus station with much traffic, touts and lively bars. We all try to find a chair but there are only three tables. But I don't have much time to ponder the impracticality of this arrangement since all the other participants have already left for a new setting by the beach. When I get there a cameraman jostles all of us into a neat bunch for a group photo. We leave a space in the middle for the Maharajah. I am relieved. Finally the symposium is about to begin. Alas! The church bells detonate. It is 5.30 am. Fuck! My plane is going down over Mechelen and I must crash land near the Brusselpoort. I steel my nerves. There is not much left of my plane, but I have not suffered a scratch, though I am a little shaken seeing all these people arrive. Distant relations invite me to an aboriginal corroboree. My Brazilian friend Nelio wants me to guide his heavy metal friend, José, up the tower of the Saint Rombouts cathedral. Laurel lights a cigarette and unveils her new film. When did she take up smoking? I find it hard to make sandwiches for all these people when I have to put my son to bed, attend these university lectures and talk to Fernando about his latest girlfriend. What is my dad doing here? Why is he wearing that pink suit? He looks at me, cracks a joke and rests his head affectionately on my shoulder. The bloody church bells go off, all at once and out of time. It is 6 am. Another day in the Barri Gòtic.

It is distracting trying to make love with all these cats jumping on us. Cats on the bed, cats on the dining table, cats stealing socks out of my joggers, pulling books from the shelves, getting caught up in the speaker leads, leaving hair on the plates, cats smelling my armpits, cats fighting, cats on heat, kittens crawling into my backpack or playing Tom and Jerry scurrying after fake mice. Cat shit and spilled cat food are scattered everywhere. For someone who once built a wall of books to keep two Siamese cats at bay while trying to sleep on Roland van Campenhout's floor after a show in Gent, these cats are traumatic. It takes skill to leave the attic with our guitars, trying to prevent the cats from escaping down nine flights of stairs. How often have I run up and down this building to retrieve a cat? We know them all by name now. Monica always begs for Kitkat. Luna hisses in annoyance at the kittens. I wish Bear would use the kitty litter. We have locked Cherio out on the roof after she pissed on Parissa's red dress. We give up on foreplay. Instead Parissa tries putting the cats to sleep by singing Dolly Parton's 'Jolene'. It worked yesterday. Perhaps we should invest in a Dolly Parton CD to revive our love life. During our afternoon siesta, in between busking stints, Luna decides to give birth. All the other cats wail while I act as midwife. Leika and Monica fight over the afterbirth while Orange, Pesto and the kittens climb all over Luna to share in the excitement. We clean up the blood and the shit. Leika bites me on the foot. Pesto breaks Lisa's expensive bottle of L'Eau d'Issey perfume. It is impossible to keep the cats under control, so I separate Luna and her fresh kitten and carry them up on the roof in a basket. But Luna is not interested in her offspring and keeps meowing all afternoon until I bring her down again. We coax the other mothers, Monica and Leika, to feed the newborn, but they too have lost interest. The kitten is left to its fate.

Barcelona is a splendid city to explore. In between busking we wandered the alleys of the Gothic quarter, in awe of Roman murals, palaces and churches, mingling with families out for a stroll in the cool evening air, lovers holding hands, a lone man singing Gregorian chants in the Carrer de la Pietat. We climbed up the staircase to the Capilla de Santa Agata, built atop a Roman wall to get a splendid bird's eye view of the old city with its church spires, towers, rooftops and courtyards. From a sun-drenched square we turned into shaded alleys that captured a welcome Mediterranean wind and smelled of freshly baked bread, fried seafood and onions, urine, ancient dust and the exhaust fumes of Vespas. Outside the cathedral elderly Catalans danced gracefully in a circle, their heads raised, clasping hands. We visited the Picasso museum and took a metro out to the Parc Güell, high on the hill of El Carmel, to chill out in the peaceful gardens, stroll among the colonnades, arches and vaults, angles and curves, columns built like tree trunks, the dazzling mosaics—all paid for by the industrialist Eusebi Güell and designed by Catalan's master architect, Antoni Gaudi. On a bench in the shape of a giant, multi-coloured sea snake we rested, looking out over the city and the Mediterranean Sea beyond.

While Parissa does her daily yoga asanas, I seek out the harbour breeze. Elegant yachts, towboats and catamarans bob on the water. In the brown grass, exiled from the sea, an old copper-coloured submarine is raised on stilts. A ferris-wheel stands motionless, the coloured horses sparkling with mirrored glass, until a chubby boy with spectacles chooses a chariot and the giant wheel starts turning, the riderless horses galloping to the shattering salsa music from the cranked-up speakers under the watchful eye of a single dad, doting on his boy. How many times have I done that?

August came. It was 36 degrees. We travelled south to Camaruga to stay in the seaside apartment of my childhood friend Frieda, with whom I had eloped when we were ten. It was a thrill to see her again. Lounging on the deckchairs of her balcony, we looked out over the strip of beach, crowded with sunbathers, brown-skinned parents dozing beneath striped yellow and red umbrellas, kids yelling and splashing in the placid Mediterranean Sea. Young men played petanque and frisbee while their girlfriends bought beaded necklaces from Malian refugees. Frieda and I rekindled an ancient friendship. I received news of people I had not heard from in decades. In just a few hours whole lives were played out before my eyes as in a picture book: births, marriages, divorces, sickness and suicides. We talked and talked, crossing the bridge of half a lifetime, over a bottle of chilled cava. Memories rolling of the reels of a black and white silent movie while, on the sea, windsurfers crisscrossed our view. A lone fishing boat plowed the glittering waves. High upon a wooden tower a lifesaver peered through his binoculars.

Parissa returned from the beach, displaying her suntan, which, at night, glowed in the dark. Her laughter bubbled like Catalan mineral water. This was her idea of a real holiday: a temporary vacuum of azure skies and lazy water, Spanish salads, friendship, books and quiet conversations. Frieda's husband Luc phoned from Mechelen with the exciting news that my friend Rombout had fixed the date for our concert at the Cultural Centre in my hometown. Bo had called my father to ask for addresses of family friends to send invitations to the show, but received an angry refusal, leaving my friend in shock. Bo had expected pride and support from my dad. Was it only me who knew that my father had been ashamed of me for most of my life? When I had announced that I was coming to Belgium to introduce my wife to the family and perform at the Cultural Centre, my dad had replied that I should just stay in the country I had chosen. His letter had felt like a dagger piercing my heart. I suddenly was apprehensive about returning home. Ten years had gone by since I was last in Mechelen, recovering from surgery at my brother's home. That night I dreamt that bullets whizzed around my head like hornets. Lost in a place of chaos and war I desperately tried to get back home, but dangerous bandits had shackled me. A duel took place, with the whole town as a witness. I woke up in the middle of the night and scribbled down a poem dedicated to my dad in Flemish, a language I had not spoken in a decade.

The time had come to leave Barcelona. The time had come to face the music. The time had come to break the glass barrier between my father and me, to dance with the bones of my ancestors once again. I treasured these last days on La Rambla. La Rambla is derived from the Arabic ramla, which means a 'sandy riverbed'. It is the emotional heart of this city and now it felt like a refuge to me. We had become embedded in this theatrical family. The Roman centurion with a golden face gave us a nod; the Egyptian mummy shook his head in time to our songs; Armando, the gypsy, stopped for a chat; the Chinese girl tinkling cocktail jazz on a Korg keyboard, the Peruvian who blew 'Sounds of Silence' on panpipes and the man with the performing dog smiled like co-conspirators when we passed by; the tattoo-artist offered us a free tattoo; waiters at the terraces greeted us like regular customers; the drunk that lived in the portal of the church who used to scream 'I love you', now said 'buenas dias'. We were tourists, disguised as exotic wildlife, who were daily filmed and photographed by other tourists on safari. We talked to them in Spanish, but understood their discussions in French, English, German, Spanish, Portuguese and Dutch, about how much they should reward us. Once more Parissa and I sang Pronto llegara, Zefinha, Sodade, Olere Camara and African skies, each of us turning to face a different table. Whole verses disappeared when the traffic lights turned green and the groaning of buses and hooting taxis took over.

'This is the story of how we begin to remember, this is…', but you never found out because the lights had changed.

Pass the hat and leave this terrace to the clarinetist or bagpiper. We had become a popular item here. Couples broke into a dance to Cravo e Canela; a Brazilian businessman offered us his card and told us to contact him when we passed through Salvador and he would organize some shows; an American tourist threw a twenty-dollar bill in Parissa's hat; a group of German architecture students voted us the best act on the Rambla and booked us for a midnight birthday party. We defied the jackhammers, drills, electric band saws, ambulance sirens and snarling motorcycles one more time and extended our busking territory to the ritzy terraces along the Ramblas da Catalunya and beneath the glow of the Gaudi lampposts, among the fire throwers, drunks, cops and tourists enjoying their cena (supper) at the restaurants on the Plaça Reial. One last time, we rescued Bear and her kitten from a neighbour's rooftop, by sliding an old plank across the narrow gap, high above the canyon below. Hand in hand we took a stroll along the promenade at night and made love in our attic among the cavorting cats. It was time to leave.

5
ZECO

THE RHINE RIVER FLOWED MAJESTICALLY PAST castles and vineyards growing up terraced hillsides. Transport barges and cruise boats with decks full of tourists glided on its smooth surface, viridian in the afternoon sun, slate grey at dusk. From the train window Parissa pointed out the picturesque churches, wheat fields and silos, villages of white houses with steep roofs clinging to forested riverbanks, crumbling fortifications on outcrops of rocks straight out of the Niebelungen. The train crept through darkened tunnels to emerge in bright daylight to yet more castles and, suddenly, to the Lorelei rock, towering over the fast-flowing river near the town of Saint Goar. We both looked up but could not see the maiden combing her golden hair on the rocky ledge high above the water, awaiting her knight's return from battle. With an hour to kill in Köln we peeked into the huge vault inside the gothic cathedral, the famous Kölner Dom, and stared at the golden shrine where it is claimed that relics of the Three Wise Men are held, or perhaps someone else's remains, sold to a shrewd bishop, aware of its promotional purposes. Beneath the flying buttresses of the

Kölner Dom, we sampled an item of German street cuisine named 'reißekuchen': battered potato mash deep-fried in oil and indigestible. At 20.45 PM we boarded the train to Belgium, and soon crossed the border into Wallonia in darkness. I peered into the night thinking about my dad.

Like most boys I worshipped my father. He was kind, affectionate, good-natured, playful, wise and just, a romantic, yet during my teens our relationship became uneasy. My father had been following my musical direction with growing alarm. I had always obtained excellent marks at school but, when I heard Jerry Lee Lewis, Ray Charles and Buddy Holly on Radio Luxemburg, I became so agape that I had to redo a whole year of high school. I formed a rock and roll band and relations became strained. It was deemed unworthy for the son of a judge to shriek Little Richard songs at parties and dances. The family's reputation was at stake. Making matters worse was my decision to stop attending church. After eleven years of Catholic schooling, I had had enough. It was the final straw for my pious father, who prayed before and after every meal and drew a cross on his children's brow before they went to bed. He refused to discuss the matter, storming out of the living room instead with a tantrum. My parents decided to put some spokes in my musical wheels, determined to get me on to the right track. The right track was laid out before me: to become an esteemed lawyer or doctor, to settle down, raise a family, grow a bank account.

— 'Money doesn't make you happy', pronounced my father, 'but it contributes a major part'.

When I had begun my law studies I saw much less of my parents. I lived in a student room in the university town of Leuven, spent my weekends in the bars and clubs of Mechelen and Brussels, and my holidays working in factories or on the docks in the port of Antwerpen and wandering around Europe with a raised thumb and a guitar on my shoulder. Though I did continue and complete my studies, my father did his best to discourage my musical aspirations. When the student union of the university of Gent offered me a show, he told them on the phone that a 'so-called Carl Cleves' did not live at this address. When, on my return from Africa, a theatre in Mechelen invited me, his response was: 'Not in my town'. I moved to Antwerpen. A musician in the family was cause for scandal. Did my great-grandfather Engelbert perhaps leave a bad smell? The voodoo of the bones of the ancestor? When I launched my first Brazilian album in Belgium my parents' advice had been: 'Please! No interviews or shows, Carl. Do it in Brazil.' My parents had never even heard me sing or play! I had become the proverbial black sheep, the bad example, the rotten apple. My love of going walkabout around the world did not help my case. Nor did my attraction to Buddhism, nor my career choice of farming the Australian bush. In Australia a 'farmer' is an honourable profession, but in Flanders a 'farmer' translates as 'boer', that means 'peasant': in my parents' ears, a backwards semi-literate character digging up cabbages on a small plot of land to survive. There are no large farms in Belgium. I could see their point of view. My mother's sleepless nights, after receiving letters from unsafe places, and my father's concerns for my future were real, but, like an albatross, I had a flight path to follow. I had met my parents on few occasions since I had hitchhiked out of Mechelen, in the snow, bound for India 25 years ago, though I had kept in contact through—now so nostalgic and old-fashioned—letters and photos. For a good while only my mother wrote to me. My memory had now stored so many terrabytes of people and places, highs and lows, that my childhood reminiscences had blurred. I was no longer who I used to be. My dad was eighty years old. Time had stretched. I felt that I didn't know who my father really was anymore. And I was probably a stranger to him.

The train ride seemed to take forever. It was a slow train, a 'boemel' train as we call it in our Flemish dialect, stopping at every little village. Belgium is a small country but there sure are a lot of villages and small towns. I felt a surge of excitement when we stopped at familiar stations: Verviers, Liege, Leuven. To while away the hours Parissa and I made up songs from the names of the stations we passed through, singing in the empty railway carriage: 'Bye Bye LEUVEN, bye bye happiness. Hello Mechelen, I feel like I could cry'. 'I'm in LEUVEN, I'm all shook up'. 'It's been a HAACHT day's night'. 'Viva BOORTMEERBEEK'. We stopped at Muizen. The next station would be Mechelen. My heart was beating faster as the train slowed on the platform from which I had begun countless journeys. Would anyone be here? It was after midnight. We stepped off the train with rucksacks and guitars, straight into the arms of my mother and father, sisters and brothers, nephews and nieces.

'Welcome to my daughter-in-law' said my dad as he embraced Parissa. My father does not speak English, but had rehearsed his line. I swallowed deep and followed him down the escalator to the waiting cars.

Belgians like to eat, and know how to eat, and over the next six weeks we were swept up in a whirlwind of dinner invitations and afternoons of coffees, cakes, tarts and pralines. My parents threw a formal all-afternoon feast in our honour with the whole clan present, nineteen of us, seated at a long table, tucking in lobsters and turbot with béchamel sauce, tossing off expensive wines and gorging on profiteroles, chocolate mousse, crème caramel, pastries and ice cream. My dad sat at the head of the table like a benign godfather, smiling on his flock. Diplomatically, no mention was made about our forthcoming concert at the town's Cultural Centre. It was the elephant in the room. The posters were all over town. We lodged at the home of my nephew Filip and his wife Iris celebrating her first pregnancy, and with my sister Denise, who has inherited the superb cooking skills of my mother. Denise remembered all my favourite dishes and spoiled us daily with chervil soup, shrimp croquettes, salmon braised in butter, steak au poivre, endives rolled in ham and baked in the oven with a cheese topping. My cousin Luc, the kindred music lover and founder of the classical record company, Phaedra, named after his daughter, drove all the way to Holland before dawn to buy mussels, fresh from the fishing boats. Old hippie friends dished up curries, wines and joints. Brothers, nephews and nieces, cousins and schoolmates—no one wanted to be left out. It was an emotional and gastronomic rollercoaster. Parissa and I were piling up the kilos.

Oh! what a thrill it was to show off my beautiful hometown to my newlywed. The town I had hurried away from without glancing back, I was now displaying with pride. Parissa, always happy to discover new places, shared in my joy as I guided her through the Palace of Margaret of Austria where my father passed judgment and the Catholic college where my brothers and I had been confined for so many years. I sneaked her inside to take her into the main hall where I had sung Gregorian chants with a large mob of boys while priests patrolled the aisles. With hushed voices we shuffled through the deserted Gothic Church of Our Lady across the river Dijle, where my brother Eric and I once posed as the performing priest's sidekicks, dressing up as altar boys and blowing myrrh, ringing them bells and singing the occasional 'Gloria' or 'In Excelsis Deus', holding the priest's robe and having a little swig of red wine, the blood of Christ before it is the blood of Christ if you know about these matters. Being altar boys was more engaging than feigning to be praying and singing with an alert priest from our college breathing down our neck, eager to catch out boys who were trying to memorise Greek conjugations from little notes hidden in their prayer books. Might as well be on stage with the priest. How I loved initiating my love into the mysteries of my past. The strange Flemish dialect that I had never sworn off now made sense to Parissa, who had always thought of my exclamations as eccentricities of my invention. When my sister brushed off a piece of fluff from Parissa's jumper and exclaimed "Ah! a plushke", Parissa burst out in hysterical laughter, hearing the word she had always presumed a figment of my weird imagination. In a marriage of different cultures nothing is more revealing than to delve into the place of origin of your partner. And by taking Parissa to the palaces, churches, courtyards, bridges and béguinages, parks and gardens, markets and shopping malls, the quiet backstreet canals and the funky cafes by the Dijle River, I also reconnected with the town where I was born.

Shows were confirmed for Antwerpen and Rijmenam, but the most challenging one would take place in the Cultural Centre in my own town, Mechelen. Parissa and I embarked on a volley of radio and press interviews. Photographers and a TV film crew lined up at the house of my sister Denise. My brother, my sister and nephews hung posters and dropped leaflets into mailboxes. Their support was magnificent. The buzz was around town. Bo, my friend and impresario for the occasion called with the news that one hundred and twenty-six tickets had been sold already, with still a week to go. From my mother and father little was heard, except for a call to my sister, prompting her to advise Parissa on her wardrobe for the night of the show, and another one to my brother, wheedling him to urge me to abandon the Rijmenam show 'because it is only a pub, and so near our town'. I decided to invite my father and my brother Eric to a game of cards in a café of their choice.

Eric and my father were the only ones in the family who didn't speak English. They had felt a little left out, when everyone else had taken Parissa into the family fold. Both were keen card players and had spent years of their leisure time shuffling decks and calling trumps in the smoky bars and coffee houses of Mechelen. 'King' was the family's favourite game. I don't often play cards and King is the only card game I know, though I have taught it on many occasions when pressed for a round. And so Parissa, my brother, dad and myself faced off, under the watchful eye of my mother, in the bistro of the same theatre that, years before, had been the cause of my leaving the town, when my father had objected to my intention to perform there. It was a lovely afternoon and there were few people in the bistro. No mention was made of the upcoming show. My father, of course, was the winner of the game. He always could remember every past move. We ordered another round of beers (my mother and brother), coffees (my dad and I) and hot chocolate (Parissa) and made small talk. My dad commented on the sad case of a twenty-year-old Nigerian girl that had dominated the Belgian media in recent days. Back in Nigeria the girl had been forced into a marriage with an older man, who had already poisoned one of his wives. She had fled the country and sought asylum in Belgium. The government had tried six times to deport her, but the girl had resisted each time, so that now even the pilot refused to take her on board. On the TV news the country had witnessed how eleven gendarmes held the girl down, gagged her and tied her up. My dad was as outraged as I was, and I recalled how, as a judge, he had always administered the law justly while keeping room for leniency, when his heart demanded so. Ethics will top any law. It was the father I adored, the idol of my youth. In a family of four children there had been few special moments of intimacy between us and this afternoon of playing 'King' was added to these precious memories.

I was gliding and soaring, backwards and forwards, high in my time machine with a cargo of emotion, discoveries and epiphanies, much laughter and tears while, behind the medieval façade and below the cobble-stoned streets of this Flemish town, a clogged artery of Parissa's bloodlines suddenly awakened and roots would intertwine. The trigger of it all is somewhat disputed. My sister Denise and my nephew Filip both claim to have stood in line behind Alex at a cash register in a supermarket in Mechelen, years earlier, when he paid his bill and spelt out his surname: 'BOUAS'. Both Denise and Filip profess to have called out: 'I have an uncle in Australia who is married to a Bouas!' The momentous meeting has become legendary now and, as all legends, it wears a cloak of mystery.

We first became aware of this fact when we received a letter in those pre-digital times—and I do not recall whether it came from Denise or from Filip—in the mail box with the puzzling news. Did Parissa Bouas, my Australian wife of Greek descent, have a relative in the Flemish town of my birth? Intrigued, she consulted her dad Dimitrios, or Jimmy, as we called him.

— 'it is possible', he speculated, 'I fled Corfu with my cousin, Fotios in 1944. Italian fascism collapsed and the occupiers withdrew. But instead the Nazis took over and bombarded the island. We had to get out quickly. I never knew what happened to Fotios.'

The two young men arrived in Naples. Fotios, who was the ex-chauffeur of the mayor of Corfu, found work as a taxi driver while Jimmy signed on as a steward with the merchant navy. He sailed the oceans of the world for many years, leaving us with black and white photographs of a dapper man posing in a white Lacoste polo shirt and pressed trousers on a boulevard in Nicosia, strolling with an elegant woman on Copacabana beach in Rio and on shore leave in the port of Panama. One day, Dimitrios left his ship in Adelaide, renamed himself 'Jimmy', and eventually settled in Sydney, where he fell in love with Frances, a curly-haired vivacious Australian woman. Parissa was their only child. She inherited her love of Latin music from her dad. A few stories, faded photographs of his large Greek family, a collection of postcards of his travels and large saffron prayer beads—his komboloi—are what she is left with. Many photographs leave a lingering question mark. What are the stories behind them? Jimmy passed away long ago. The cousins never saw nor heard of each other again and the enigma was shelved.

Until years later, while on this first European tour with The Hottentots, Parissa and I were invited to dinner at the house of Edith Lambert in Mechelen. Edith and I are old friends. A gifted artiste, she drew the cover image for my first EP recorded while on a wander in Germany during my student days and she had cared for me in a time of crisis. Over an entrée of escargots, exploding in garlic sauce, Parissa told the cash register tale when Edith exclaimed:

— 'But that must be Alex Bouas! He was in my office this morning. Let me give you his phone number.'

Thus began the remarkable story of the reuniting of a severed connection to blood, language and culture.

We met Alex the following evening in a café on the Grand Market square over a chilled glass of Kriek, a Belgian beer fermented with sour cherries. Alex had brought his partner Bie, his sister Marise and brothers Aristotelis and Michael. All of them had married Flemish partners. We sat by the window, looking out over the illuminated 14th century Belfry and the Lakenhal, nebulous and mysterious in the drizzling rain. Alex is a boisterous lad, a can-do man with a big heart in a broad chest, a deep-sea diver, a great cook and a jack-of-all trades, who earned a decent living as a plumber and house painter, repairing roofs, chimneys, central heating systems and laying floors. He would try his hand at anything. Welding sculptures, playing saxophone, name your craft. No dream is unattainable in Alex's mind, and his stuttered command of English was no impediment to a lively conversation. He spoke his mind and you knew you could trust him. His sister shared his joviality; the other brothers did not speak any English and listened. Parissa and

Alex exchanged family histories, while Marise and I translated for the brothers. Parissa was the first member of the Bouas clan they had encountered, outside of their own immediate family. When their father had arrived in Belgium, intent on integrating, he had renounced his Greekness, stubbornly refusing to ever talk to his children, hungry for information, about his background. How Fotios Bouas ever journeyed to Flanders no one knows but what is certain is that he left his children with an aching question mark. For all those years they had lived in a void. Where were they to dig for their roots? A dank fog hung over the Grand Market square of Mechelen, but this serendipitous reunion lifted the cloak of mystery of their past, exposed their ancestry long buried under the sands of silence. The chance meeting with Parissa turned their lives upside down.

It caused a revolution for Alex and the Flemish branch of the Bouas clan and a grand journey began for them. Parissa brought them into contact with their many relatives in Corfu. Within months, Alex and Bie visited the island. Alex, Marise, Michael, Bie and Ari learned to speak Greek and enrolled in weekly Greek dance classes. They travelled to Greece each year and connected with the large Bouas tribe. We received photographs of them in traditional Greek costumes. Alex has now bought an apartment in the old town of Kerkyra and spends his days between Mechelen and Corfu. Bie, the Flemish wife of Alex, has since become a learned teacher of Greek dance, even giving workshops in Greece itself. The shield of the Bouas clan that he brought back for Parissa hangs in her office in Byron Bay. The Flemish branch of the Bouas is reunited with its roots, and Parissa has not only been welcomed into my family, but into her own Corfiot family as well, in the town of Mechelen. At our first concert in the Cultural Centre of Mechelen, there would be, besides my friends and family, twelve relatives of Parissa in the audience.

Nine AM and it was still dark. Autumn had come suddenly. It was raining outside and, lying in bed, I flashed back to my school days, crawling from beneath my toasty eiderdown into the chill of morning to run to the Church of Onze-Lieve-Vrouw-over-de-Dijle, bitter cold and bleak, to attend 7 AM mass. Then I suddenly remembered: today is the day of our show in Mechelen. Denise had already set the table and the smell of fresh coffee, gurgling in the percolator, wafted up two flights of stairs. On CNN Bill Clinton was denying his affair with Monica Lewinsky with a smirk on his face.

— 'He's just a naughty boy!' quipped Parissa with a grin.
— 'Did you sleep alright?' asked my sister, always concerned and obliging. 'The Cultural Centre will be packed tonight.'

I buttered my croissant and thought of all the people that would be coming to this show, some whom I hadn't seen since childhood: old college friends and teachers, geriatric aunts and teenage nephews, lovers of classical music and pop, the plain curious ones, doctors, lawyers, judges, friends of my parents. How to satisfy such a diverse crowd of people?

My parents had bought tickets. The scandal would be worse if they didn't turn up. This was the first time in their lives that they would hear and see me perform. Perhaps they feared I would enter on stage with a nose bone and a mohawk, red leather pants and a flying V electric guitar, fall on my knees and scream 'Fuck the police! Fuck the pope!' like they might have accidently seen on MTV.

Tonight will be just fine, I told myself.

The house lights were dimmed. Video cameras rolled. The poet, Francis Verdood, had composed a glowing, and over-blown, introduction. You could hear a pin drop. Parissa gave me a V sign and we stepped on to the stage with the opening riff of *the Last train home*, a song in 7/8 like a wake-up call:

'It must be sorcery, I must be dreaming
I could swear I hear the whistle of a train

Tell me can you hear someone screaming
This is your chance, it won't come again.'

Train songs have always given me a rush. They are the start of a new journey. A promise. Orange Blossom Special, Wabash Cannonball, Chattanooga Choo Choo. Panama Ltd, Midnight Special. Names like mantras. Freight trains, fast trains, ghost trains, big trains and blue trains, morning and midnight trains, peace and freedom trains, salvation and hell bound trains, gospel trains, devil's trains, trains that rode 500 miles or 900 miles, six or twelve coaches long. Train songs are great concert starters. Get aboard! Each performance guarantees a train ride to a different destination. Each day of our life is a departure.

'Taking the last train, taking the last train, taking the last train home!'

The applause was reassuring. I had prepared introductions and stories in Flemish, pronouncing long forgotten dialect words like secret passwords, chewing them like caramelized fruit. Playing a gig is like swimming across a river. After the first frisson of the cold splash all you must do is move your arms, paddle your feet and trust that you will get there. I felt comfortable performing with Parissa. After all, we had shared the stage hundreds of times before, in much more difficult circumstances: sick with flu, one of us voiceless, hostile audiences and crappy sound systems. But this night the Flemish audience was with us, hanging on to every word, every note, laughing at slapstick banter, tearful with songs of the heart, falling in love with Parissa, even joining in on the tongue-twisters of the zany title track of our latest CD *The Voice of your Heart*.

'Yalala yelele leyaa! Yalala yelele leyaa!' sang my eighty-year old dad with everyone, rising to his feet. I dedicated the song of *Zeco*, a prisoner on death row, to my parents and sang it like a whisper, holding back my tears:

'The judge said I give you a life behind bars
That is what you deserve for your crime
How I wished that I could
Hear your voice one more time'
(Zeco)

We returned for several encores. Parissa received a bouquet of roses and the curtains fell. We stepped into the barroom like Christians entering the lion den. The den was packed with people wanting to felicitate us and reminisce about times past. Here was my feeble seventy-six-year-old high school teacher in his black soutane; the photographer who, by chance, had shot the sessions of my first record in Belo Horizonte; and the cook who served the Belgian consulate in Johannesburg and with whom I had lodged, while the consul was on leave. Some well-wishers had become rich, some were divorced, some suffered tumors, some were alcoholics. Friends whom I had once hobo-ed with introduced their wives. Schoolmates with whom I had shared a desk in primary school looked me in the eye and quizzed: 'do you remember me?' It was an emotional and overwhelming experience. Bo, my faithful friend who had organised all this, was beaming. His daughter and her boyfriend served the drinks at the bar. My sister Denise and brother Luc, his wife Monique and my nephews sold CDs and passed them to Parissa and I to be dedicated. My two brothers drove us back to the house of my sister when it was all over. Our heads hit the pillow at 3AM.

We slept until midday and woke up, still glowing from the events of the night. Telephone calls with congratulations came in all through the afternoon; one of them was from my parents. As always it was my mother who was the mouthpiece. My father did not find it easy to express his emotions.

'Your father and I would like to congratulate you and Parissa on a fabulous concert last night. You are both artists with a capital A. Your father is proud of you.'

From that day on things changed between my dad and I. Perhaps his image of the wayward son was dented. 'Artists with a capital A', he had declared. In Flemish culture artists are allowed and expected to be different, to be eccentrics who do not play by the rules of a bourgeois society. After all, what is Flanders famous for if not for its painters and poets, sculptors and woodcarvers, composers and tapestry makers. The prodigal son had been welcomed back into the fold. In the coming years Parissa and I would visit Mechelen regularly, performing in the 15th century Palace of Margaret of York, now the City Theatre, in the Theatrium, the rock venue where had I once played dances with my teenage band, The Dragons, and other venues.

I received the news of my father's death in Melbourne. Parissa and I had just landed at the airport from a tiresome tour in South Australia when my brother Luc called. We made our way across the city to Reservoir where we would mind the house and two cats of our friends, the musicologist Joseph Jordania and his wife Nina who were visiting family in Georgia. Parissa had to rush off to coach a couple of community choirs while I remained alone in the house with my thoughts. An intense feeling of isolation, sorrow and regret overwhelmed me. Nothing was worse than to be so far away from the rest of my family who were grieving together and consoling each other. I sat for hours at the kitchen table staring into space. When I stood up I had a dizzy spell and collapsed, my face hitting the corner of the table. I must have been unconscious and came to in a pool of blood. The kitchen was a mess and I tried to clean it up, but not well enough, giving Parissa a shock when she came home.

When I visited a medical centre the next day the Greek doctor told me my face was too swollen to have a diagnosis and sent me home. I had two black eyes, my nose and lips were badly swollen. When I visited the clinic again two days later x-rays were taken. My nose was broken and after the weekend I would have to go to hospital. Parissa and I travelled to northern Victoria where we played two shows. The audience reacted with horror to my entrance on to the stage with a deformed face. Cracking a feeble joke about having run into a door did not get a laugh. I was a mess, breaking out into tears out of the blue, but not on stage. I avoided the emotional songs, choosing the lighter and irreverent ones instead. When I finally got to the hospital I was told that, as a week had gone by since the accident, my nose had set and would have to be broken again. Well, I had my nose broken before by a young bull, and didn't feel like going through it all again. The doctor told me that since I could still breathe through both nostrils I would be able to live with it. My father's funeral was held in the Church of Onze-Lieve-Vrouw-over-de-Dijle, the same one where I had been an altar boy. The church was packed with family and well-wishers and my song *Zeco* was played during the service. I heard the news from my sister ten days later.

6
RECYCLED GENES

WHEN BOTH OUR PARENTS HAVE PASSED AWAY we realise that we are next in line. It is now too late to ask questions, to try to understand, fill in the missing pieces. There is more I don't know about my parents than what I do know, yet I carry the genes of both of them. Perhaps I look more like one of them, but relate more to the other. But how would I know, without travelling in a time machine to witness how their lives evolved from birth to death, their hidden thoughts, traumas and aspirations? What about my ancestors who contributed their DNA to my parents, and as such to mine as well? Animal studies suggest that our behaviour can be affected by events in previous generations, passed on through a form of genetic memory. A Nature Neuroscience study shows that mice, trained to avoid a smell, passed their aversion on to their 'grandchildren'. Is that what the partisan nightmares of my youth were about—or just early memories buried deep?

And isn't our whole human family tree not interconnected? The dictum 'we are all one' is factually true. In 2004 mathematical modelling and computer simulations by a group of statisticians led by Douglas Rohde, then at the Massachusetts Institute of Technology, indicated that our most recent common ancestor probably lived no earlier than 1400 B.C. and possibly as recently as A.D. 55. In the time of Egypt's Queen Nefertiti, someone from whom we are all descended was likely alive somewhere in the world. We are all somehow inbred. Is that what oriental philosophies suggest when they talk about reincarnation? Are the failed composer, Engelbert, the tough and suffering women with golden hearts, Veneranda and Maria, the army officer that fought Napoleon, my disapproving father, my mother so easily moved to tears, my operatic granddad with the sweet tooth, embedded in my being? Are they an essential part of who I am? Have they returned to live within me? Are all of them recycled as I will be? 'For dust thou art and unto dust shalt thou return', so tells the Book of Genesis. Are lessons to be learned over generations, as the theory of karma insinuates?

7
BIENVENUE

WE LEFT TULÉAR IN STYLE AT SIX AM, CUSHIONED in the comfort of an air-conditioned four-wheel drive Toyota that was returning to Antananarivo. Most tourists who came south rented a private car with a driver, and flew back from Tuléar to Tana. The driver then tried to hustle passengers for his return journey—at a cheap rate. Seeing the arid landscape roll by from behind a thick, glass window screen was a diversion from sweltering in an overcrowded taxi brousse, dust blowing in, speakers cranked up, bumping to tsapiky hits. Parissa and I were on the antiseptic tour, watching a muted TV documentary from a lounge chair. There was little life along the road to Sakaraha: scrawny, low shrubs with purple flowers; prickly pear cacti; red termite mounds; baobab trees like Roman pillars. No arable land. No zebus. Only elaborate, brightly painted tombs and a village of midget-size, grass huts. In the middle of the Route National 7, Madagascar's main artery, two geese refused to budge. Our driver graciously veered around them. Before midday we reached Ranohira and got out. We were back at the base camp of Isalo National Park. The second time around.

Momo is a large Comorian with the moustache and winning smile of an entrepreneur. He is also the proprietor of Momo Trek, providing basic bungalows and porters, equipment, tents and provisions for excursions to the nearby park. It is a funky, but efficient operation, and he wanted to expand it. Studying a map over coffee with condensed milk, Momo sat beside us in his bar/restaurant, when a gust of hot wind swept the map from the table. He bent down. Over his shoulder, an expanse of long silvery grass, bare of trees but for lone flat-topped acacias, moved with the wind, like waves on the ocean, like clouds in the sky. It reminded me of the endless plains of Serengeti. A wall of sandstone cliffs marked the far horizon.

At the Angap office—the government organisation that manages all fourteen Malagasy parks—we arranged with a young Bara man to guide us on our treks in the park. His

name was Bienvenue. Samby Bienvenue. He spoke little English, but good French; was short of stature, more a youth than a man. We left immediately for a twelve-kilometer walk under the smoldering midday sun, marching through the plains of parched grass until we reached the eroded massif. There was no shade along the way. Sweeping views over barren valleys, ancient riverbeds and steep canyons—the remains of a Jurassic world long gone. Crumbling towers of mustard-yellow sandstone, horizontal erosion lines jutting out like a skeleton's ribs; craggy pinnacles, guarding the patches of dull green along the streams like sentinels.

'Vontaky' said Bienvenue, pointing at a bulbous mini baobab, blown up with a bicycle pump and dressed up gaily with pretty yellow flowers.

He looked at his booklet and read 'Pachypodium rosulatum'. While Bienvenue named the outlandish plants that survived between the eroded rocks I questioned him about Bara history. What better opportunity for a lesson than a long walk.

History of the Bara people according to Samby Bienvenue.

The Vazimba were the original inhabitants of Madagascar. They were a little, pigmy-like people. From the coast of Mozambique, the Bara, an African tribe, set out in large pirogues across the ocean. They arrived on the west coast of the great red island and did battle with the Vazimba. The Bara won, spread out inland and formed three kingdoms. Bienvenue himself was a family member of the king of the Barabe—the large Bara. He scraped arrows in the sandstone track to illustrate. Our pathfinder was in his early

twenties, rather delicate in stature, even though he was related to the king of the large Bara, but mucho simpatico—a little reticent as Malagasy often are at first meeting. One should not start a conversation by barging through the door. A gracious and mellow approach is preferable. Decorum forbids loud behaviour, arguments, rudeness. But beneath his unassuming manner Bienvenue had a royal bearing. We would be spending much time together.

We came to a splendid waterhole, fed by a waterfall, in a small oasis of cycads, pandanus and palm trees, and jumped in.

— 'You have not heard any music of the Bara?' asked Bienvenue, drying in the shade of a rock.

I had been telling him that we had come to Madagascar at the invitation of Hanitra Rasoanaivo, leader of the band Tarika, to connect with musicians and to study and document the rich traditions of the island. We had shared a concert in the capital and had been travelling through the highlands, the south and northwest for two months, filming and recording among the Merina, Sakalava, Betsileo, Mahafaly, Vezo and Antandroy. He started singing a tune.

— 'What is that song, Bienvenue?'

— 'A song about stealing zebu.'

Whereas the highland Betsileo and Merina are rice growers, the much darker Bara are herdsmen. They like their zebu, the long-horned humped cattle, introduced on the island around 11th century by South Indian Tamil merchants. Even though the Bara practice polygamy, cows are often closer to a man's heart than women. The worth of a man is measured in zebu. Zebu-rustling is a popular activity. It is

considered cool for a young man, about to be married, to impress his in-laws by stealing someone else's zebu.
— 'Last month the police shot ten zebu thieves here.'
He sang another zebu rustling song.
— 'There are many songs about that. Kilalaky music is based on them.'

We resumed our trek past reddish aloe cacti growing between the rocks and descended into a valley of sand. Blunted spires and cragged cones of rust-coloured stone, rose from the hillocks. We stopped to look.
— 'There are also thieves of graves. They rob the graves for the silk lambas in which the bodies are wrapped. The lambas are very expensive.'

He pointed at the wall of sandstone, teenage pink and burnt orange in the gilded afternoon light.
— 'That is why it is better to bury the dead in the caves and hollows, high up the cliffs. That is where our King Valitera is buried.'

He told us that there were also some Sakalava tombs here, rumoured to contain treasures.
— 'But the Bara have driven the Sakalava out of these lands.'

I learned much that day, as Bienvenue explained the inheritance practices among the Bara, the workings of Angap, the proper Bara names of the instruments used in a famadihana (the traditional reburial ceremonies), the antsa songs dedicated to the ancestors. We arranged our next walk to the canyons for the following day. I wrecked my eyes that evening, filling my diary with notes, under a fifteen-watt light bulb.

We woke up from a rough sleep. Our bed base missed a vital board and the mosquito net was slightly too short. Malagasy furniture and gadgets are wonky. You turn a tap or shower hose, to be left with the thing in your hand. You follow a promising pipe but it is not connected to anything. Loose wires and fittings abound. Beds have one short leg; tables and chairs wiggle. Pillowcases are stuffed with rough straw or prickly grasses. Much of rural Madagascar seems to be patched together. We washed clothes in the shower. The breeze was hot and dogged. Clothes would dry quickly. Drying clothes was usually easier than washing them. Buckets and sink stoppers were missing. There were regular water restrictions and sudden power blackouts. Many hotels did not allow washing laundry in bathroom sinks. I hung my jeans out to dry on the electric wires.

'Pas de problème', said Momo, 'the generator is only switched on at night'.

Bienvenue led us across the golden plains of grass to the canyon of the Makis. It was a long and dusty trek. In the densely verdant canyon, black-snouted, silver sifakas swung from the trees, garbed as fluffy masked marauders—the Zorros among lemurs. Small red-breasted thrushes skittered between the shrubs. Bienvenue pointed out couas, bul-buls and coucals, while continuing his dissertations on Bara customs. He himself had lived in a small village nearby and studied Bara culture with the king. Loosening up, he told us about his studies in Fianarantsoa, how he had fallen in love with a girl at school, with whom he was now married. They had a four-year-old son, named Tafita. We set out for the Canyon of the Rats. Parissa was exhausted and preferred to rest at the gateway. Bienvenue and I continued ambling up the canyon.

Kestrels flew up from the satrona palms, kingfishers skidded low over the pools of clear cool water and up against the salmon coloured rock face. The Canyon of the Rats is a spectacular place. We climbed and clambered up through narrowing chasms, vertical walls on either side, swam in chilling water and ate our lunch on a tiny beach of white sand. I told my new friend a little about life and landscape in Australia and milked him of Bara lore. It was there that our guide confided that, later that week, the famadihana of King Valitera, the last son of King Tsimangataka, king of the Barabe, would take place. I told him that I would be interested to witness the reburial since it was one of the reasons I had travelled to Madagascar. Nothing more was said about it. We started on the long march back in the fierce afternoon heat. By the time we reached Momo Trek Parissa had blisters on both feet. I shouted my friend a beer and we bid each other goodnight.

When Momo learned that we were musicians and had performed in the capital with Tarika, he asked his porters to play some music for us that night. The guys arrived while we were struggling with a supper of tough zebu. They set up a drum kit—a crash cymbal and a turned-up bucket—in the corner of the bar. Soon they were strumming guitars and singing kilalaky songs. I never got to finish that leathery zebu steak. Parissa hobbled off to get her katsa and, for the first time since leaving Tana, I wished I had my guitar with me. Without guitar, and having lost my voice, all I could do was copy the moves of the porters and dance between the dining tables with Gloria and Hanta, the two bartenders. Hanta was a beautiful soul with a melting, sad smile. She had been giving my beloved a crash course in Bara dialect. Parissa and Hanta had become good friends; she wanted her as a neighbour. We raged for hours while a savage wind blew in from the desert, pushing over the saltshakers and toothpick holders and lifting the red and white chequered tablecloths. But it was the dancers that lifted the roof off the shed. Tsapiky, salegy, mangaliba, kilalaky—even some sentimental ballads. We rocked our breath away with circle dances, couple dances and acrobatics of the African variety, each of us jumping in the circle to demonstrate what legs, feet, hands, hips and arms are really meant for. Even Parissa stomped on sore feet.

While Parissa nurtured her blisters, I strolled into the village of Ranohira the next morning hunting for food supplies for our treks. I felt like Elvis ducking out of

Graceland to buy a hamburger at the corner shop. Everyone greeted me with a smile and the women in the zoma giggled when I wished them 'nario coua' in Bara lingo. These little explorations always gave me a cheap thrill. Men were loading up zebu charettes. Women, bearing enormous bundles of grass on their heads, sidestepped a taxi brousse whizzing by on the route national 7. In the school the children burst into song. Shopkeepers peered at passers-by. Everyone had time for a chat. Mora mora. Slowly slowly. Conversations were unhurried. It is good manners to take care of greetings and small enquiries before coming to the matter at hand. I acquired four tiny tomatoes, half a dozen bananas, a packet of biscuits, two bottles of water, two mini baguettes and the big prize: a packet of butter and a little block of local cheese. I ran into Bienvenue. He was with another man. We made small talk. He had a gleam in his eyes.

— 'I must come and see you this afternoon,' he said. 'Four o'clock?'

Bienvenue arrived like a boy coming home with a terrific school report. Hanta served us coffee with condensed milk. Outside the Isalo Massif shimmered in a blazing haze. Porters were idling away the hours on the porch.

— 'Did you see the man who was with me this morning?' he asked.

I nodded.

— 'That was the king,' he announced, looking at me to await my reaction.

I wondered why he had not introduced me—but establishing intimacies takes time in Madagascar.

— 'I have asked the king for his permission to take you both to the reburial ceremony of his father, King Valitera. Permission has been granted', he said pompously.

Over the next hours Parissa and I received detailed instructions—'information we should know'—and planned our journey. Bienvenue, now not our guide, but the royal man he really is, explained everything with thoughtfulness and clarity. We must leave no later than six am and walk to the Canyon of the Makis. Just after dawn the villagers would have removed the corpse of the king from its provisionary grave in a cave high up in the rock cliff, where it has been stored since his death one year ago. They will arrive with his remains about the same time as us at the settlement of Ranohirabas where the festivities will begin. There will be speeches. He taught me the oratorical sentences I will have to say to the king and reminded us of the small donation I must offer the king in a sealed envelope. We would have to bring food, a tent and bedding—because there will be a multitude of people descending on the village and there is nowhere for us to stay.

Until well after sunset I sat with my friend taking notes of the order and significance of the rituals, the duties of the participants, the song cycles, the etiquette we had to adhere to. He warned us that many people would be drunk, to be wary of the homebrewed rum and careful, especially at night, since many tribesmen were armed. Famadihanas are the most important expression of ancestor worship in Madagascar and the village had saved up for a year to celebrate the event. For the Malagasy mindset the ancestors—the razana—have never left them and must be honoured. Their offspring will be blessed in return. The festivities would run over three days. The actual reburial, after the bones of the king had been washed in herbs and wrapped in new silk lambas, would take place on the third day. The bones would then be carried by a group of men who must climb up the rock wall and redeposit King Valitera in his new tomb. I told him that we could only participate for twenty-four hours since we were expected back in Antananarivo for an important music festival. We shook hands in the traditional manner, holding the right wrist with the left hand. He blurted out that he had a surprise for me.

— 'Demain', he said with a mysterious grin, 'tomorrow.'

The weather changed. A bitter gale blew in from the Massif. The sky was the colour of a gravestone. Slate-grey clouds concealed the canyons. I shaved outside in the snarling wind—only a trickle of cold water to share with a thirsty bug-eyed chameleon and Parissa, who was washing socks. Someone was axing firewood somewhere. Momo Trek was deserted. In the street men and women were wrapped in blankets. Hanta arrived, carrying baguettes. Soon there would be coffee brewing. The wind cut right through the bar, tablecloths flapping like flags. A chilly mist of rain sprinkled—one could hardly call it rain, but rain was rare here—and then the sun showed up, letting the shadows of the windswept eucalypt trees dance on the red soil. The bent-over gardener was raking leaves. We often met people collecting leaves, especially in the national parks. Leaves to cure diarrhoea and stomach aches. Leaves to settle fevers. Leaves to make rum. Locals were permitted to collect leaves from national parks. Only a few days ago, at the

Canyons of the Makis, we had met two women cutting foliage.

— 'To make rum', Bienvenue had told us.
— 'From some trees it is fady—taboo—to cut the leaves. They can only be collected from the ground.'

Many unforeseen things are 'fady' in Madagascar, like swimming in a particular lake, walking past a special tree or eating a certain food. The rules of fady change from place to place. In every zomba there were stalls selling herbs and little clumps of wood, used by the ombiasy to heal sickness. I could have used some of that too; I wasn't feeling so good. Must have caught a chill.

I had just organised the rental of a small tent and sleeping bags with Momo when Bienvenue turned up. With a glowing expression he handed me an exercise book with a picture of the Eiffel tower on its cover.

— 'This is a present for you. For our friendship', he said shyly.

It was a booklet with his handwritten notes, taken during his studies with the king. I looked at the first pages of neat handwriting in blue, red and black ink, his drawings of the Bara instruments and his additional notes in French. I could not believe that he had given this to me. I was really moved and hugged him.

— 'It is fady to pass on this information, but the king has given me special permission. '

We sat down together and leafed through the pages. Here were detailed day-by-day descriptions of famadihana practices among the Barabe people; descriptions of bilo or spirit possession practices; formulaic, ritualistic sentences with their French translations; pages on the antsa chants, the soheo songs of the young women, the jihèa songs, chanted by the children of the deceased during the reburial ceremony.

I went back to bed after my friend left. I was running up a fever. It had started raining again. I was trying to remember when we last had real rain. There was nowhere to escape from the cantankerous wind, but in bed. Parissa snuggled beside me and we slept all afternoon. It was still drizzling when we ate duck and rice in the piercing, piping gusts at Momo Trek's bar/restaurant. We were the only guests. Rivulets of rain ran over the red earth, making the paths muddy and sticky. The Massif was blanketed with ominous black clouds. Hanta promised to prepare sandwiches for the journey tomorrow to Ranohirabas. I went to sleep in feverish anticipation, the gale howling through gaps in the door.

8

DANCING WITH THE BONES

BIENVENUE ARRIVED AT SIX AM SHARP AND WE SET out at once under a granite sky. A chilly breeze bent the reddish grass, but for large areas of scorched earth where zebu herders had burned the land. The Canyon of the Makis remained out of focus, cloaked in the morning haze of rising vapours. Our guide was keyed up. He reminded us of the protocol we needed to heed, sang and translated the ceremonial songs we would hear later that day, and explained the roles of different family members during the famadihana. We learned how King Valitera had died at the age of 112, without ever having taken western medicine. The king had left seven wives behind—and countless children, grandchildren and great-grandchildren. Until recently the village of Ranohirabas had been located within Isalo national park, but Angap had enticed the king to move his settlement in return for a donation of land, the building of a community house and concessions. The Barabe would continue burying their ancestors within the boundaries of the park, use its river and plant resources and retain some grazing rights. The new Ranohirabas nestled at the base of the sandstone cliffs. On our approach we could hear the crack of gunshots.

Bienvenue led us straight to a whitewashed brick building with a brand-new corrugated iron roof in the middle of a cluster of huts of russet mud and thatched roofs.

We stepped through the open door, adjusting our eyes. The community hall was packed tightly with people sitting on the ground—women on the south side, to the right, men to the left. All eyes looked up. Treading over many bodies we reached the front, where two men sat beside a sculptured wooden box on which lay a large bundle wrapped in a blanket of pink and indigo stripes—the coffin and the bones of King Valitera. We bowed before the men. I gave my envelope to the one I presumed to be the king and recited my condolences. Bienvenue translated my request to witness and film the famadihana. The king addressed me. He was unshaven, hulled in a blanket, indistinct from the other men. He thanked me and welcomed us to the village. He then directed himself to the gathering.

— 'He is telling them to treat you as honoured guests and care for you while you are in his village. You will be considered part of the *vavarano* and enjoy his protection. Vavarano means "the ones who drink from the same river", the immediate family of the deceased.'

People shouted their approval and one man, squatted against the wall, shot his rifle through the open window.

— 'He shoots his gun to ward off bad spirits from the bones of the king', whispered Bienvenue.

The king spoke again.

— 'You can film everything except the sacred lambas, the coffin, the tears of the widows and the actual reburial.'

Bienvenue had explained to us that it was the role of the widows to weep and lament. The grandchildren were expected to taunt them, accusing them of having wanted the death of the king. Following my friend's suggestion, I asked permission to be exempt from drinking the rum. I lifted my t-shirt and showed the scar of the operation on my abdomen and, pointing at Parissa, added that my wife suffered from a fever. Permission granted, Bienvenue and I squeezed between the menfolk on the ground. Parissa joined the women. She was wearing a lamba over her jeans. It was the proper thing to do.

We remained in the hall for several hours. Male orators spoke and Bienvenue mumbled explanations in my ear. There were proverbs of wisdom and traditional discourse, while cups of rum were passed around. Feuds were settled before the king. A drunken, one-eyed man beside me kept pestering, pushing me and grinning with his toothless mouth. I did not understand what he was saying, but he suddenly stood up and went to sit with the women. Freeze! All the women regarded me. On a gut instinct I pointed at the man and made a firm gesture, ordering him to return to my side. When he did, the women yelled their approval and broke into song. They sang and clapped hands for almost an hour. Some women kept quiet, with solemn expressions. I presumed they were King Valitera's widows. After a while people started drifting in and out of the hall. Outside a man had set up a shonky sound system, powered by a car battery. A group of children hopped to the music, thrusting bent knees from side to side and swinging their arms. Adults left the hall to join in. Women danced cradling babies. Young and old stomped, while two girls went around with a bucket and a cup, offering rum. A woman, hair braided close to the scalp, her face covered in masonjoany paste, grabbed Parissa by the arm and they started shimmying. Though I was filming, I too was pushed in to the dance. It was obvious that we could not simply be observers. We were expected to be full participants in the famadihana.

Parissa and I stood out like goats among a herd of zebus. No one was quite used to the presence of two vazaha. Except for Bienvenue, we could not converse with anyone. Smile and boogie was all we could do. A woman with an amber coloured headscarf, tassels swirling about her like the queen's dreadlocks, mocking eyes lit up by a grand piano's beaming row of teeth, moved in on me. She had found a lump of wood, the size of my camera, and followed me around, imitating my every move as I filmed—until I cracked up and danced with her. I had never rocked so much as in Ranohirabas. Over the twenty-four hours we spent in the village the dancing never stopped—day or night.

Soon everyone got used to us. Accepted as part of the scenery. Inside the hall a teenage band of kabosy players was hotting up. A drunken man, eyes glazed, shimmied in the middle of the seated crowd, his bare torso shuddering, his groin pulsing to the relentless rhythm. A child handed him a cup of hooch. It was not even noon and many people were intoxicated. But what at first appeared to be a delirious, drunken chaos, revealed a framework of set rituals and well-organised responsibilities. It was the duty of the sons of the deceased to protect his remains. It was the task of the grandchildren to dance continuously. Some men slaughtered zebus, others brought and axed firewood. Kids were on rum duty. Women carried water from the river; others pounded rice in wooden mortars. A dozen women sat around four large, iron cooking pots—'aligned according to the tradition', said Bienvenue—tending the fires and sieving

rice in woven grass pans, tumbling the rice with a swing of the arm and throwing it up to the rhythm of the music blaring from the one speaker.

Things were going on in several places at once. One minute we were clapping in the hall, the next we were dancing outside. A man had collapsed in a drunken stupor. I presumed he must be one of the grandchildren whose duty it was to keep on dancing. A spirited group of women encircled him, singing and clapping, urging him to get up. One called out, the others responded. They chanted in unison. They whooped and shrieked when a girl jumped in front of the drunk, her lamba wrapped around her thrusting pelvis, her black eyes rolling, wholly mocking him. Another girl followed. Then another. They kept at it until finally the man staggered up, supported against the mud wall of a hut. Someone gave him a cup of rum and a cigarette. Then he tottered, wobbled and started swaying again. The famadihana had only just started. He had another two days to go!

More and more people arrived in the village and the commotion intensified as the day wore on. Inside the hall, unflagging women were singing and clapping antsa. Outside everyone stomped on hard clay to the DJ's limited choice of Malagasy hits. Cattle herders who had come from far, blankets round their shoulders, baseball caps and hoods, rifles at hand, leaned against the huts, drinking and watching the mayhem. There was nowhere to escape in this small village—but for the communal, open-air toilet shrubs, just beyond the perimeter of the huts. I strolled over to the corral where zebus were chewing their cuds, fenced in by branches and thorn bushes. Behind them the rose-coloured

escarpment of the Isalo Massif looked spectacular in the fading light of day. Bienvenue found me musing. As we walked back, a frenzied mob scampered past us, chanting and jeering, to disappear among the huts.

— 'Ils chantent des gros mots', explained Bienvenue.

This was the song cycle of abusive and dirty words, the jihea songs. Shots went off, ricocheting from the walls of the massif.

The decapitated head of a zebu lay in the dust near the cooking fires. Veins dangled from its bleeding neck. Two women were cutting up the red meat on an empty rice bag on the ground, throwing chunks into the pot with bare hands. A dozen or more women sat near the fires, infants at the breast. Chickens ran among it all and someone kicked a dog that was trying to grab its share of meat. The DJ was back. He had mounted a spotlight on his table of crates with a recharged battery. There was no electricity in Ranohirabas. Night was descending.

Bienvenue dragged me from the dancers.

— 'My mother is inviting you to come and eat with our family', he said, 'but first you must mount your tent. It is almost dark.'

At his suggestion, we put up our tent behind his mother's hut, at the edge of the village, near the corral.

— 'So we can keep an eye on you', he joked.

The silver-coated capsule looked like an alien spaceship amid the mud huts.

— 'Your mother has a great view over the massif.'
  'But it is the most dangerous position', he retorted.
  'When the zebu rustlers attack, they target the huts nearest the corral.'

He showed me the holes, cut in the walls of the huts on the periphery.

— 'To shoot at the rustlers', he said.

It was so dark in the hut we could hardly see how many people were inside. Beside his mother's bed, there was no other furniture and everyone hunched on the ground. Lea, Bienvenue's heavily pregnant wife, sat beside us, her son Tafita on her lap. Lea and Parissa had been hanging together all day. They had become buddies, though they did not share a language. Bienvenue introduced his mother, his grandparents, sister and brother Harson, and an elderly, drunken uncle, who must have had some bad experience with vazaha, as he kept hanging over me, slurring in Bara slang. There were no bouncers in the joint. A small metal dish with bits of zebu was put in front of us. Parissa began chewing. I could not face it; put a small chunk in my mouth, and secretively, but adroitly, spewed it into my hat. A single, teeny-weeny can with a kerosene wick was the only light. No one noticed. Parissa suffered from parasites over the next four months. When we were finished the rest of the family dined on what was left over.

— 'Stick close to me', admonished my friend.
'Many people are not used to these vazaha being around. They are drunk and it is dangerous for you in the dark.'

Indeed, several fights had broken out, including with the soundman who had suddenly packed up his system. I couldn't discern a thing and kept bumping into drunks. Gunshots, fired to invoke the ancestors' presence, pierced the night. A numbing desert wind swept through the village. A frantic mob circled the hall, singing and shrieking. Inside, the kabosy band was ablaze. People crammed on the dirt floor, the flickering shadows of two kerosene lanterns on the walls. In a dark corner three men strummed never-ending riffs at breakneck speed. A drummer hit a plastic bucket, a tin can and an aluminium lid stuck on top of a stick. Beside him two boys worked the big bass kabosy that lay flat on the ground—one beating the box with his fist, the other sliding his thumb across two strings. The fishing wire must have worn off the skin, because his thumb was bandaged with a rag. Another two days to go. A fat, bare-chested fellow with a red cap, sunglasses and dirty shorts was shimmying and shivering in the middle of everyone—a cup of rum in his hand. Others lay against the walls, wrapped in blankets, staring. King Valitera, the life of the party, witnessed the celebrations in his honour from a silken bag on the lid of his coffin. I recorded, filmed and danced. In the smaller, adjoining room the rave party was pumping to the band. Through the open door I saw Parissa shaking and seesawing among a packed crowd of dancers, young and old. Now and then I caught Bienvenue from the corner of my eyes. My friend was guarding over us.

I woke up with a jolt. Parissa lay sleeping beside me. The kabosy band had stopped. Somewhere in the night men and women were singing. Their chants drifted, now closer, then further away, weaving between the huts. One man called, the others responded. It was powerful. It was rousing. I clambered out of the tent. The night was freezing cold and dark as the inside of a sock, the feeble Milky Way, frozen in the sky, the only faint glimmer of light. I found my way to the outdoor kitchen fires and saw them. Some twenty men, women and teenagers, ran past me, ululating, and disappeared among the huts. The next time I saw them they pulled me with them, and we began to run circles around the hall, shrieking and singing.

— 'To protect the bones', Bienvenue had explained, 'they must do it all night to keep evil spirits away from the bones of the ancestor.'

Trying to find my way back to our tent in the dark, a man slouched over me and wouldn't let go. He was terribly drunk, mumbling and rasping in my ear. I couldn't get rid of him, so I dragged him with me to the hut of Bienvenue's family. I called my friend softly, though I am sure that my drunken attachment would have woken everyone up already. Bienvenue came out with a torch, shining the man in the face. He became very polite, gently talking reason into the man, I presumed.

— 'What does he want?' I asked.
— 'It is the king', said Bienvenue.

Oh me oh my! Thank God I hadn't removed him by force. He didn't look like the king of my memory.

— 'This morning you addressed yourself to the king's secretary', clarified Bienvenue, 'the king was the other guy.'

The king interfered and started slurring, still holding on to me.

— 'A gun' said Bienvenue, 'the king wants a gun'.

I was perplexed. I had no guns. It was four am. What was I doing here negotiating an arm's deal with a king?

— 'Would he settle for five thousand ariary', I asked.

He did.

Parissa had woken too. There was a hint of light in the sky. Together we returned to the hall. Everyone was still singing and hollering. The heavy bag with King Valitera's bones was hung from a stick and hoisted on a strong man's shoulder, while all around him clapped hands and stomped feet in wild abandon. He ran out of the hall into the crisp light of dawn—all the others in tow, chanting and ululating. Parissa and I, of course, raced behind the king's bones with them, through the alleys of the village, and out into the dry red country, cantering breathlessly, laughing, whooping and chanting, sobbing and crying.

The rising sun gilded the tall grasses as we scampered back into the village, where young and old were romping, garbed in jackets, blankets and bonnets. The bones were swapped from one shoulder to another. The soundman had reappeared and we shimmied in the chilled desert air, singing along with the kilalaky songs we had heard, again and again, honked from the speaker. By now, even Parissa and I knew

the Malagasy refrains. Two grinning women jived around her while the clowning camera lady with the amber headscarf, looped between them, bent over, the hefty bone bag on her back. Kids were weaving around with buckets of rum. Seesawing to the rhythm, I fend off a drunk. I jerk and I lurch, leap and swerve behind the king's bones, feet stomping on the hard red soil, smiling at everyone, with tears streaming down my cheeks, dancing with the bones of my own ancestors, Engelbert, Theresia, Veneranda, Lodewijk, Maria, Albert, my parents, whose genes I carry, the arthritic knees and inflamed intestines, the love of music and words, the passion and endurance, my parents gentle hearts, our failings and our strengths. I could lay them all to rest. Soon I would join them too—as will all those who danced around me—to our common roots deep below the clay. The intense emotion and explosive energy of the last twenty-four hours found release. We had been in a state of high alert. During the famadihana the rest of the universe had ceased to exist.

A swarm of women and children were huddled by the fire on grass mats. From a simmering pot, a woman scooped out cups of hot rano vola, the rice drink made from boiling water in the burnt remains of yesterday's rice. The one-eyed, toothless man asked me to take a photograph of him with his family. I had let him photograph Parissa and me, as we were dancing with King Valitera's bones. Someone offered me a chunk of zebu. I declined. I was starving, but could not stomach zebu so early. There was much smiling. Smiles of encouragement. Though we did not know their names, gleaming eyes and bouncing limbs had made the

connection. We had a shared a momentous ritual. People had been generous with us; the women protective towards Parissa, making her feel safe. We had danced and sung together, most of the day and the night. I had filmed everything and everyone, unstoppable, high as a kite.

Two boys carried a freshly-slaughtered zebu head by the horns and put it in the dust. Its dead eyes stared at the fire. It was time for us to leave. I felt sorry to miss the following days of famadihana—especially the last day when Bienvenue, his brother and other men would face the daunting task of climbing up the vertical rock face of the canyon, carrying the casket with king Valitera's remains, wrapped in a brand-new silken lamba, and rebury it in the cave tomb.

— 'We must take up a jug of five liters of rum and drink it during the climb', said Bienvenue. 'It is very dangerous.'

He led us before the king for a ceremonial farewell. The king did not seem to remember our nighttime encounter and courteously invited us to return, declaring that we now belonged to Ranohirabas, that there always would be food and a place for us here. We strolled around the village and went into the hall, shaking everyone's hand in the traditional manner. Taking leave of Bienvenue and his family was the hardest. Hours after leaving, the constant kilalaky beat kept pounding in my head. We both felt exhausted and delirious. The long journey to Antananarivo passed like a laudanum dream.

Two months after returning to Australia I received a letter from Bienvenue. The famadihana had ended in tragedy when his brother had fallen while climbing up the steep canyon of the Rats to rebury King Valitera's remains in his tomb.

'He broke his head, cut his arms and died', my friend wrote.

Then he gave me the good news. His wife Lea had given birth to a baby boy. They had named him Samby Mbahionjo Harson Carl.

'Samby was my father's name; Mbahionjo is a blessing; Harson is the name of my deceased brother; Carl: no comment.'

MADAGASCAR GLOSSARY

Angap:	Association Nationale pour la Gestion des Aires Protégées; the organisation that administers Madagascar's national parks
Antsa:	traditional rapping and clapping vocal style
Ariary:	Malagasy currency
Fady:	taboo
Famadihana:	reburial ceremony
Hotely:	small informal restaurant serving basic meals
Kabosy:	square-boxed guitar with partial frets. Also called mandoliny or belamaky
Katra or katsa:	shaker made from a tin filled with little stones, attached to a handle
Kilálaky:	popular music derived from the Bara zebu rustling songs
Lamba:	cotton or silken sarong, worn as a shawl or over skirts
Masonjoany:	face pack made from wood and water
Mora mora:	slowly, slowly
Ombiasy:	healer
Pousse-pousse:	rickshaw
Rano vola:	rice drink made from boiling water in a pot containing burnt remains of yesterday's rice

Salegy:	electric danceband music in 6/8, originating from the Sakalava people
Sifaka:	type of lemur
Taxi brousse:	bush taxi
Tsapiky:	fiery electric dance music from Madagascar's southern regions
Vazaha:	foreigner
Zebu charette:	the wooden-wheeled carts pulled by zebus that are Madagascar's traditional form of transport
Zebu:	the cattle of Madagascar, a national symbol. Zebu have wobbling humps on their backs and flaps of loose skin hanging beneath their throats. The flaps allow better heat regulation in arid areas; the humps store fat
Zoma:	market

ABOUT CARL CLEVES

Carl Cleves was born in Mechelen, a traditional Flemish town in Belgium. He graduated in his Belgian Law Studies and was offered a scholarship to study traditional African music with ethnomusicologist John Blacking in southern Africa. This started off many years of travel throughout Africa, the Middle East, the Orient, the Pacific Region and South America, guitar in hand, acquiring musical skills and an endless supply of stories and songs. His adventurous life has included stints as an antelope trapper in Uganda, relief worker in cyclone struck India, foreign correspondent and ethnomusicologist in Africa and night club crooner in the South Pacific. While living in Brazil he became a popular singer and bandleader.

He is the author of *Tarab: Travels with My Guitar*, an epic tale of high adventure and the search for musical ecstasy (TransitLounge.com.au). His six solo albums and six with The Hottentots, co-founded with his wife Parissa Bouas, have won international praise and numerous awards, including Music OZ, NCEIA and ASA: 'Songs both intimate and powerful'; 'a vision whimsical and wise'; a guitar style 'utterly captivating, pregnant with unexpected nuance'.

'Carl Cleves reminds his readers that true travel is about sinking deeply into cultures and allowing unique experiences to change your life'. Bruce Elder (Sydney Morning Herald)

www.carlcleves.com
www.facebook.com/CarlCleves
www.youtube.com/carlcleves

contact: carl@carlcleves.com
Byron Bay NSW 2481 Australia

Tarab. Travels with my guitar—Carl Cleves

Transit Lounge Publishing

'By any measure, Cleves deserves to be mentioned in the same breath as Thesiger, Burton and Newby. He is an astute observer, a passionate participant and a man prepared to undertake interesting, but never crazy, experiences.'

'Cleves is a rarity. He is a true traveller in an age of holidaymakers and gawpers. He heads out to experience the world and reminds his readers that true travel is about sinking deeply into cultures and allowing unique experiences to change your life. The result is a journey that enriches Cleves and the reader.'

Bruce Elder – Sydney Morning Herald

'This is much more than a musician's memoir. It is a beautifully written and well-researched narrative revealing the philosophical, political and emotional journey of a man and his guitar traversing different cultures, extraordinary characters, near-death experiences, deep friendships, ill-health, a successful recording career, and perhaps the most enduring terrain of all, parenthood.'

'This is a book to curl up with and be transported to other places and other times. The intimate tone gives the reader the feeling of listening to the melodious lilt of a magical weaver of tales. The rich prose is filled with images that will stay with you long after the last page.'

Laurel Cohn – Byron Shire Echo

'Thanks heavens for Carl Cleves! As Director of the Byron Bay Writers Festival, my days are long and opportunities for travel rare. Through Tarab I have been thrust headlong into an extraordinary tour of wild times and wilder places. I have laughed, gasped and loved every starling page, courtesy of this insanely talented man'
> *Jeni Caffin* -director Byron Bay Writers Festival

DISCOGRAPHY

- *Before Twilight Turns to Night* 2018 (Australia)
- *Haloes round the Moon* 2014
  (Germany - with Parissa Bouas - Stockfisch Records)
- *The house is Empty* 2012 (Australia)
- *Out of Australia* 2010
  (Germany - with Parissa Bouas - Stockfisch Records)
- *Tarab* 2008 (Australia)
- *All Alone* 2007 (Australia)
- *Turn Back The Tide* 2004 (Australia with The Hottentots)
- *Graceful* 2001 (Australia with The Hottentots)
- *The Voice of Your Heart* 1998 (Australia with The Hottentot Party)
- *A Small World* 1994 (Australia with The Hottentot Party)
- *Love is a Phantom* 1987 (Brazil)
- *African Lion* 1984 (Brazil)
- *Come Enter my World* 1966 (Germany)

'The missing link to the classic UK folk scene from the 1960s.'
Folkworld

'A real feast for the ears.'
Alternative Music Press

'Amazing songs. An original variation on folk and world music.'
Sydney Morning herald, *Bruce Elder*

Carl never ever tries to sound like anybody else. He has managed to absorb these other influences while retaining his own muse. An uncompromising artist with a personal vision that is both whimsical and wise and yet he's not averse to injecting a bit of hokey fun into the proceedings. His melodies are memorable and moving. Carl's acoustic guitar playing is utterly captivating and pregnant with unexpected nuance. In fact Carl is the only acoustic guitarist in Australia whose work I can detect after two notes. His sound is that singular. Yet he never grandstands.'
   Diaspora World Beat

www.ingramcontent.com/pod-product-compliance
Lightning Source LLC
Chambersburg PA
CBHW021943290426
44108CB00012B/938